BEYOND THE WALKAROUND

A New Vision of Modern Automotive Sales

Robert J. Hamilton

Hamilton Sales Training

Rockford, Illinois

BEYOND THE WALKAROUND

By Robert J. Hamilton

©2014 by Hamilton Sales Training.
7431 E. State St #144
Rockford, IL 61108 USA
http://www.hamiltonsalestraining.com

ISBN 978-0-6923-5256-4
Library of Congress Control Number

TABLE OF CONTENTS

Acknowledgments i

Introduction 1

Create the Environment/Set the Tone 19

Preparing For Purchase Consultation 41

Feigned Indifference/The Technique 65

Addressing Price Concerns 83

Trade-Ins 113

Payments 147

Putting It All Together 167

Lead Management and Follow-Up 185

Conclusion 205

Index 211

ACKNOWLEDGEMENTS

This has been a wonderful and fun project. I have had hundreds upon hundreds of relationships during the many years I have been in this business. The majority of these relationships have been good or great. This book has much to do with the experiences others have provided for or shared with me. I have always continued to study and learn from everyone. The belief that no single person in a dealership is more important than another (only levels of responsibility differ) has enabled me to grow from all with whom I have had the pleasure of working. Thank you to you all.

A few of the fine consultants I have worked with during my career are mentioned in this book. Almost everyone, though, is part of a collection of fond memories. The ups are treasured, the downs respected. Thank you to all who have been a part.

My thanks are now in order for a new group of consultants, who by purchasing this book and participating on blogs and websites are truly a part of my professional family. I am truly appreciative of any and all support.

I want to thank my family: My mother Barbara, who always provided love and encouragement; my sister Deb, who has given consistent inspiration; and particularly my father, Roger Hamilton. He has been a source of great support and encouragement for as long as I can remember.

But, nothing could have been done without the devotion and support of my wife, Nicole. Thank you for that and for putting up with me!

BEYOND THE WALKAROUND

INTRODUCTION

Thinking back through the nearly twenty-five years of my career in the car business, there are a great number of memories that move in and out of my mind. A bit funny maybe, but I can't help but remember my first attempt at a product presentation. It seems to be more clear than most. I really don't know why, yet it makes some sense and it is the perfect theme from which to launch this fun and unique journey you and I are about to take. The subject of the presentation was a Caprice Classic. It was unfamiliar to me except for the specifications, features, advantages, and benefits that I had crammed into my brain over a short period of time. But, I had these things and a single note card to help. The prospect was daunting - my attempt, relatively feeble. The showroom was enormous. It could attractively display 18 vehicles on the ground and the thirty-foot ceiling that was nearly all glass, more like a gigantic atrium really, provided not only the room for banners and additional point-of-purchase material, but perhaps also for maybe the most awesome acoustics ever in an automotive retail facility. All of this meant to me was that *everybody* would be able to hear me. And what they were able to hear was a pretty run-of-the-mill regurgitation of the specifications, features, advantages, and benefits. Of course, it was to be expected of a first attempt. Over the early part of my career, I became pretty good at these walkarounds. I became less rigid, created more excitement, had more emotion in my voice, and was far more sensitive to tailoring the event for the customer.

There were a few bumps in the road, to be sure. Even a couple of years into my career, I was young and immature, with all of the neat things that go along with that – the impetuousness, the over-confidence, etc. There was a morning one summer in the middle of the week, I think it was 1993, when we had a sales meeting where the staff was scolded pretty strongly for not performing consistent and meaningful product presentations. It was costing us car deals and gross, the message went. And, aside from the manner in which this point was made ("scolding" perhaps not really covering it), if we were not taking care of such basics all of the time, every time, we were indeed costing the store units and dollars. At any rate, I kept this fully in mind when I greeted a man and his five-year-old son a bit later in the morning. He mentioned that he had some interest in the new Lumina (in case you hadn't gathered, I started in a Chevrolet facility). Rather than do things the proper way - attempt to bring the guest inside the store, build some rapport and comfort, and then conduct a quality interview/needs assessment - I instead flew into action. All of the vehicles then were equipped with lock boxes, so I was able to open a vehicle up right away. I hopped in the Lumina, light driftwood in color with a light interior, and pulled it forward. I was taught to separate the vehicles from the others, increasing customer focus and allowing the room necessary to show the entire vehicle without hindrance or distraction. And so, with the man and his young son standing a few feet behind me, I began the presentation. The Luminas were displayed running along the front, opposite of customer parking and within direct view of the sales desk and showroom. Well, I knew I had an audience, a couple of managers and sales consultants alike, maybe the greeter too.   Within seconds I had the hood, trunk, and all of the doors open. Then, for five minutes, I proceeded to enthusiastically give the walkaround of my life, arms waving, voice inflecting, and, well – what a show! I knew that this was exactly what my managers were talking about, and I wanted to make sure that they knew I wasn't one of those giving poor presentations. And so, I went on. I became lost in my own little world. When I came out of it for a moment to ask the customer a question, I turned to find no one there. I looked in a different direction and, to my horror, he was walking away and almost to his vehicle. He was far enough away that he might not have heard me had I yelled, which of course I didn't. At least I knew that much. I completely lost the customer. The humiliation began to grow. I imagined the audience watching the customer become fed-up or disinterested or both and start to walk away, leaving me to my over-the-top, ridiculous attempt to prove something (not sure what really). I put the vehicle back into line and went inside to take whatever was coming to me. I'll let the speculation begin, but at least I wasn't fired. The point, in part, is that walkarounds are important, but they don't represent everything. The other part of the point should be obvious: please do not choose the role of a buffoon as I did. This book is not about my experiences entirely, however, and we will keep them relatively few and far between; although, the self-deprecation is a bit purifying for me, and hopefully amusing to the reader.

The idea that the product presentation is not the "be all-end all" in our profession is certainly not difficult to comprehend, but it will become even clearer as we move forward. This being said, I do remember the multitude of Ride and Drives that I have attended over the years. Like some, I was not a huge fan of waking up earlier in the morning to meet and then drive a couple of hours, maybe more, to stand for four additional hours, then drive back, and work until 9 PM. Always a long day. Though, circumstances always changed for me once we arrived. These Ride and Drives are regularly set-up with actual driving, comparisons between the relative performances of your vehicle and the competition, and classroom time. These stations opened up a lot of eyes. Granted, the representatives that gave the presentations were professionals and knew the vehicles inside and out. They were enthusiastic, clearly excited about all of the wonderful new features and benefits (advantages, too) that had been added to the vehicles, providing us with a certain upper-hand when selling against our competition. These professionals, I recalled later, drew me in, made me feel excited. I thought about how much better my closing ratio would be if this type of vitality and expertise were delivered through my walkarounds. I thought about how the customer might be so enthralled that they would not have to shop and compare. The customer might buy my product right now. Then I thought: "Isn't that what I'm supposed to do every time I'm with a customer?" Why don't we have the energy and excitement level that these people do? Well, part of it is that they get paid to simply provide the quality presentation. We must do that and so much more to sell and deliver a vehicle, which, of course, is how we get paid. We have to get past this, though, to be the best we can be. The good news is: most of us can.

But, as the title indicates, this book is about so much more.

As important as product knowledge is, there are few nuances. It is what it is. It is readily accessible, easily memorized, and put into practice. How the knowledge is utilized is far more important. Learn from the aforementioned professionals and channel their energy. A magnificent walk-around can take a customer out of the market. More importantly, though, is that a single instance that creates **_discomfort_** for your customer can put them right square back into the market and not at your facility. If a consultant is not able to counter concerns quickly and effectively, customer comfort can decrease rapidly. So how do we keep customers on the road to the sale? How do we stoke the fire that we have created with our quality presentation? More importantly, for those customers who do not have time for or have an immediate desire for such a presentation, how do we even get to the walkaround? After this introduction, there will be little mention of product presentation, or a service-walk, or a proper delivery, or why these steps are so vital. The main objective will be getting you to all of these things.

Here are a couple of things you can count on with respect to the content of this book: You will not be given exact formulas for success which make no sense, cannot be measured, and are, therefore, useless. This being said, there will be ideas and concepts quoted and defined for that which they are supposed to stand or define. And then we will speak of them honestly. So, please forgive me for quoting the Pareto Principle (I find most "principles," along with fairly colorful charts, graphs, and diagrams to be gobbledygook in most cases and pretty worthless), in which many dealerships find that 20% of the staff does 80% of the work. And so, if even somewhat true that the minority of the staff does the majority of the work, why are solid performers in this business so difficult to find? It brings up an interesting point that was made when someone asked why we don't have more top-notch, highly educated individuals in this business. The reply was something along these lines: "Well, maybe most of your Harvard and Yale graduates aren't telling their parents that before they consider law school, medical school, or rocket science, they really think that the car business should be given a try." Makes sense in some manner, I suppose. Though, I have long ago decided that intellect is never a factor in defining value in a human being, and I would never dismiss the many bright and talented people we have in this business. We simply need to develop more of those individuals. Sometimes, it takes time to see the light. It has been said that there are many millionaires who are complete idiots and there are geniuses who reside in gutters. We will focus on some differences. Here is an initial step we can take…

We need to expect more of ourselves: study, learn, and practice on a daily basis. And, above all, smile and wave at every customer we see. Make their day! Make everyone's day. We can do this. Even when it is difficult, be prepared to interact with these people. I recall some time ago when a newly hired, but experienced, sales consultant called a customer out using some old-school style tactic better left for dead. The customer stormed out of the building, clearly upset and not likely to return. I asked the sales consultant what happened and he said, *"Hey, this is the car business…"* Well, not anymore. *That "car business" needs to be eliminated permanently.* So how do we do it? Follow me...

Why Beyond the Walkaround?

Now, more than ever in the history of our profession, the sales consultant must be highly-skilled and highly-trained in order to compete for the fewer positions available. This is a highly positive state of affairs, and this is a wonderful time to either be in the business or to be breaking into the business. But, you'd better come ready. Because those who are, will be able to take advantage of a market that is far less watered-down and make more money than their predecessors. Welcome to Beyond the Walkaround: A New Vision of Modern Automotive Sales. In this book, we are going to focus on some of the basics, as well as vital, though seldom-used, nuances of the business. But, we are not going to attack them in the same old, run-of-the-mill, "road to the sale" format. In fact, this book can be not only a great introduction into the overcoming objections and concerns area of your field, but also a final piece of the puzzle. You will be introduced to the innovative and ground-breaking Technique that utilizes a consistent and highly-effective blueprint for closing directly off of objections and concerns. This book is unique and the emphasis is on those concepts and skills that matter most.

The concept for "Beyond the Walkaround" was born well over a decade and a half ago while I was working at a One-Price store – don't worry though, this book is written to relate to all selling philosophies. Anyway, at that time, I observed my sales consultants consistently using the word "no" to answer a question pertaining to a discount, the price itself, or any type of negotiation. Very few of our employees were trained to handle concerns and objections properly. There had to be another way, another idea. The idea is pretty simple: have something else to say. Tell the customers what you *can* do for them, give options, or explain why something is the case without a negative slant. It's not easy, but ultimately this practice will make everyone a lot more money.

Now, you will find that this book might just be the most valuable investment you have ever made for your career. Why? Because it's designed especially for you - the automotive sales person. This is not for real estate agents, not for insurance agents, not for shoe salesmen. Not only will you find this information refreshingly different, but it comes with a full understanding of just how difficult your job in your field has become. There is more competition, there is more information out there, and technology has helped add to your lists of responsibilities and knowledge requirements. Before now, basic sales training told you what you should do, but not necessarily how. It has given you the destination, but not the map to get there. This material, along with your natural skills, will provide you with a little more help to get it done. And basically, it all comes down to your confidence and how the customer is treated. The more confident you are, the more comfortable your customer will be. In fact, that's the simple secret of the car business, and, for that matter, sales in general: Keep your customers comfortable and your salespeople (employees) confident. So how do we get there? This business has always been long on planning and strategies and short on actions or tactics. Together, we will act and get things done. Most importantly, units delivered and increased customer satisfaction. Now, with this in mind and knowing how crucial confidence is, what exactly is it that would make all salespeople more confident on a daily basis? The answer is simple: knowing how to interact properly with your customers and, most importantly, knowing what to **say** and do in response to virtually any concern in any circumstance that could arise, all the while increasing comfort.

Introduction to The Technique

So, how do we handle concerns and objections? For most, we have been taught to follow a structured response. You've heard this before: Empathize, Repeat, Write Down (if you can), Re-phrase, Head Nod, Ask for Clarification. Then come up with something. Most sales training has taught something similar: Listen and Empathize, Isolate, Provide Options/Info, Ask for decision, and Continue the Sale. Many different methods are taught through many different sources. Surprisingly, they're not all that different. All of them are solid and effective ways to make people *believe* that you are listening and care about them. You will note that empathy is mentioned in both, but true empathy is not as important as understanding. Understanding is different from empathy in that you don't really feel the way they do, but you know *why* they think or feel the way they do. Also, **isolation**, long thought to be so vital a step in the process, **will happen naturally** as you respond to concerns or attempt to move on or close the sale. In fact, the whole goal of The Technique, again explained in-full in this book, is to have your customer respond either with an "I understand" or "What do you mean?" These responses will allow you to close immediately from the "I understand," or close directly from a counter in the case of "What do you mean?" This will be repeated and expanded upon several times. So, our refreshed process will be this:

Once you have listened attentively and understood the concern, you will pause, smile or nod (or both), maintain a pleasant expression and remember to not take the concern personally, you will do the following:

1. **Counter/Response**

2. **Analyze Customer Reaction**

3. **Close or offer a 3rd party example.**

4. **Analyze Customer Reaction**

5. **Close or Retreat/Pullback**

6. **Counter/Response**

7. **Repeat as necessary**

This is known simply as The Technique. We will revisit this later and thoroughly after we have some word tracks under our belt. Now, to remind everyone exactly what this book is all about... It's not an all-encompassing sales program laden with long-winded, trivial stories that don't always make a point and which you could take or leave. This program is about setting people up for the close and making sure you effectively **ask** for the sale **every time**.

Word Tracks and Scripts

Now, a lot of books and programs offer what you might interpret as rigid, canned scripts that aren't very effective or thought-out and never seem to come off the way they should. But, even if they could be effective, most of the time they are not.

One reason for this is that other materials do not mention the importance of **rate**, **inflection**, and **tone**, not to mention the expression on your face. You will not believe the effectiveness of your words with slight adjustments in these areas. Another reason certain scripts don't work is simply that they're not used, or not used correctly and with the proper follow-up. But, we read them, maybe study them for a while, then we go back to wingin' it. What's more, these scripts are frequently too long and do not possess the pure impact necessary to create a change in thought or viewpoint. In this book, you will learn some word tracks that will. Now, please understand that I was once one of those people who couldn't stand the idea of word tracks or scripts. I thought they were all canned. I thought they would take away my individuality. I thought my managers were trying to make us into a bunch of robots. I was so opposed to the idea because no one took the time to help me understand. They didn't help me understand that the value is in the security and the new air of confidence that I would have in all situations. And, as far as the individuality goes, if a golfer alters his swing to mimic another more successful than he, if a ballplayer changes his swing to match someone who has no holes in his, if an actor emulates the technique of proven professional, no individuality is lost. The identity comes through in how these different people master and utilize the skills they are developing. You will always be you. Your delivery of the word tracks, the particular timing, is all yours. Don't lose sight of this. Can you imagine the confidence you will develop as you learn to put together a plan for what to say and how to deliver the words? And, yes, you're the one that has to do this. With the help of these things, you will develop consistent responses that will maximize your confidence and your customers comfort level. You will find yourself hoping a customer has a concern just so you can help them understand. And every time you do this, your customer will be closer and closer to buying the vehicle from you. It's a mind-set change. Think about it, though. What do we do now? What do we say when a customer asks if we'll take $500 or $1,000 off the price of our car? What if they ask if that's the best we can do? Do we stutter or hesitate? Do we say, "Are you buying today?" like many of us have either been taught or just picked up on our own? Do you tell them you have to check with your manager? Or do you just say "no," particularly if you believe you're down to nothing. Even if you say, "I can't" or "I don't think so" or "There's no way they'll go for that," you're still saying "no." If this is the case, even at times, you will learn that you don't have to say that all-too-powerful and negative word "no." And yes, it is fully understood that most salespeople would prefer not to say "no." But even if you're accustomed to saying, "Let me check with my manager!" before you have given any kind of presentation or built any value at all, you know that the "no" is coming. This book will provide a number of effective alternatives. We all know customers hate to hear the word "no." We can feel it. *We* don't like to hear it, either from the customer or from our manager or from anyone else for that matter. Noted speaker Steven Wiley

(Look him up, by the way. And see him if you can. He's fantastic) equates saying "no" to slapping a customer in the face or providing a knee to the stomach. Every single time. We must learn not to say "no." Of course there are extreme situations (it would be foolish to use the words "never" or "always" in this case), but we are going to focus on the 95% of the time. The main focus must be to let your customer know **what you can do rather than what you can't**. Also understand that this material is not meant to replace product knowledge, which is vital, particularly now, or to short-cut the road to the sale. It is designed to be a necessary supplement. In fact, you will be able to use the Technique *with* product knowledge on the road to the sale. The material in this book will actually enable you to pull your customer back onto the road to the sale should they stray. This material will allow you to take or regain control of the situation. These ideas and word tracks will sell you cars where you wouldn't have before. The key, though, is consistency. Most of us have been given various ideas about when to respond, but do we use the knowledge every time? Do we try to close or ask for the sale every time? Or do we use it or attempt to close only when the customer seems receptive? We'll study more of this later when the concept of Feigned Indifference is introduced. But, what we will do first is talk about the type of environment that we would like to set or create in our store for our customers. Why? Because your customers will respond better to your words if they are comfortable with you and the facility.

Now, with respect to our words, if you want more than "If I could, would you?" or "What do I have to do today to sell you a car?" you are in luck. Understand that there are times and places for these questions, but that time or place is nowhere near the beginning of the sales process or before we have countered not a single concern nor overcome an objection or two. At best, all these questions do if used improperly, is sell us a car with low gross or, at worst, turn a buyer into a shopper. How do we turn a buyer into a shopper? We do it by so devaluing our product that the buyer now believes there might be more in the way of a discount than we can give or that somehow he or she can buy it for less elsewhere. This will be re-visited and expanded upon a bit later.

What to expect...

There has never been so much vital and effective information wrapped into such an efficient package as is done in this book. As stated before, this is for the automotive sales consultant. But, **everybody** in the business, up to sales management and including ownership, will benefit from the material presented in Beyond the Walkaround. There are still many dealerships across the country that operate without the professionalism that is necessary for improving the business and moving forward as it evolves. What we will discover here, in this volume, will take us wherever we wish to go.

In *Create the Environment/Set the Tone,* we will learn how to create the **Customer Comfort** and maintain it. We will go over preliminary word tracks which will qualify (not pre-qualify) our customers and move them into the proper initial stage. We will be reminded not to talk about ourselves, but to learn to hang on every word your customers have to say and why this is important.

In *Preparing For Purchase Consultation,* we will learn about pre-emptive strikes and positive-value statements. We will go over **Set-Up or Transitional phrases** which lead to **Closing Questions**. Remember, we are always closing on the current step in the sales process, not just the complete sale itself.

In *Feigned Indifference/The Technique* we will learn to maximize the impact of our words. We will examine why the concept of Feigned Indifference is perhaps the most important there is, and why it is not utilized nearly enough. It is invaluable and we will talk about how one discovers the idea and how we use it. The Technique, defined earlier, can be used over and over again. We are able to close/ask for the sale repeatedly without high pressure or decreasing customer comfort. It is unique.

In *Addressing Price Concerns,* we will become acquainted with some of the most effective words we have yet seen or heard. We will counter many, many different objections and concerns with respect to both new and used vehicles. We will continue to practice **countering, transitioning, and closing** on each step of the road to the sale.

In *Trade-Ins,* we will attack what many sales consultants argue is the most difficult part of the deal. We will go over the proper preparation, how to slow the customer down a bit, and we will learn counters to **16** trade objections! The great news for everyone is that, no matter what your process (and there can be many, I know), this section will make you far more successful. You will make more deals, hold more gross, and take in more trades for the right dollars.

In **Payments**, we will counter **9** payment concerns! We will learn how to get past interest rate questions, as well as outside banks and credit unions.

In **Putting It All Together,** we really get into some fun! We'll take a look at delivery – rate, inflection, tone and such. Then, we'll go into the write-up and presenting numbers. There will be a couple of mock scenarios provided to better our understanding of how this all works on a collective basis. We will look at a section called **Famous Last Words**, which gives us *exit strategies,* if necessary. More than this though, it gives us the tools to *regain control* of a customer who is ready to leave. Once this is done, we will discuss how to, once again, make every attempt to close the deal.

In **Follow-Up,** we study newer ideas and tactics to maximize our efforts and increase our chance for be-backs, repeat business, and referrals. We utilize all available to us today, from e-mail to Facebook and twitter, and from blogs to texts!

Complete this and your confidence will soar!!

And now I leave you with this...

I have worked in a number of facilities in my career (less than most, I would imagine) and I have seen and heard a great many things. I have experienced those who do it right, and those who, most assuredly, do not. If you have not heard the old adage: "Buyers are liars," you will. And yes they are. But, so the perception has been with us

16

for a long time. It doesn't need to be so. We are able to successfully conduct business on a professional, honest platform without the deceit that has long been associated with the car business. The ideas, strategies, and tactics presented here in Beyond the Walkaround will make anyone far more successful (with respect to dollars, reputation, community, what have you) than any other, more traditional, practices possibly could. So please enjoy a shot of adrenalin to your career! Should be a blast.

BEYOND THE WALKAROUND

Create the Environment and Set the Tone

"Comfortable people spend thousands of dollars; uncomfortable people tend to wait."

A few years back, maybe more, it seemed that Disney began to expand its influence with respect to training and performance. Reaching out to other companies and offering to sell the tested and proven philosophies that had made Disney a unique success was something we saw more and more of as time passed. Many companies, GM was one with which I had personal experience, have been paying a goodly sum for a bit of time now. Of course, it should be noted that while the ideas and concepts are solid, the model is certainly not comparable. Clearly, General Motors will not eliminate all facilities in favor of two massive centers located on opposite coasts of our nation. Nor would they, or could they, staff the center with the cream of the crop of performing employees and force all customers to take a trip, perhaps stay a week, in order to purchase a single, let's say, compact Chevrolet. It also seemed as though Disney was not comfortable with former employees cashing in on inside knowledge.

Prior to the ramping-up of Disney's training endeavors, and in the summer of 2005, I had the opportunity to attend a seminar that featured Dennis Snow. This all-day event was devoted solely to customer satisfaction. Dennis spent the majority of his career at Disney and co-wrote the book Unleashing Excellence, a fine work that I recommend very highly. Anyway, as most of you know, Disney is all about the experience. One major idea that I took away from this program was that we are always on-stage. This seems obvious, and most of us might have heard this somewhere before, but it's not necessarily about acting, although there's a bit of that. But, it's more about creating the character which we would like to be at work, a character that is simply the best of ourselves, and staying in that character. Dennis joked that he had actually seen Cinderella smoking a cigarette and complaining about the "little rug-rats." He supposed this was fine behind the scenes or underground, but what kind of catastrophic effect would it have on little Johnny or Jenny as they see Cinderella in this light. Their parents might have saved for years to go on this trip only to see the fantasy crumble before their eyes (this example or one similar in nature has been used at the more recent Disney presentations). But, this is why Disney is so strict about this. And this is why we should never be seen out of character at our facility. Everyone must be aware of this. I vividly remember a situation at my store when three sales consultants were verbally going back and forth on one another at a computer desk up front. The only problem, besides the negative banter, was that there happened to be a customer hidden behind an awards board. Well, I knew what the salespeople were doing, they knew what they were doing – innocent enough. But, I'll bet the customer now standing aghast really didn't get it. Unfortunately, I could see the mouth drop open, I could see the eyes widen (there was no foul language, mind you, just unprofessional behavior), and I couldn't do anything at the time that would help. Jumping up and running out of my office to address the situation, loudly or softly, would still add to the customer's discomfort. What did he think of us now? Was he waiting for a vehicle to be pulled up for him? If so, could this cost us the deal or gross? Of course. Was he waiting for his car to be done in service or taking delivery of his new vehicle? If so, could this affect the results of our survey in the case of a new car, maybe taking us from completely satisfied to very satisfied or worse? Could it prevent us from selling another car to a used car customer? Could it hurt our opportunities for a strong referral? You bet. **The things we are not aware of are those that will hurt us the most.** We are in a fishbowl in a dealership. There is a lot of glass around. People can see us all the time. They can read expression and body language, not to mention inadvertent outbursts, large or small.

I remember goofing up myself. Anyone who knows me will tell you that I am not very fond of machines at all. And, apparently they have no love for me either. At any rate, I had been making copies and got a paper jam. I fixed the jam only to find out that the source of the jam had been, you guessed it, the last piece of paper. So I had to fill the doggone thing too. I didn't go crazy. I didn't cuss either, which was a bit of self-control for me. But, I would have clearly appeared to be irritated by anyone who might have seen me. I realized this too late. Luckily, when I looked around, there was no one there to see. Just this little reaction might have been enough to make someone uncomfortable enough to wait on their purchase. So, what do we learn from all of this?

The most important thing you must initially accomplish is to **build comfort in your customers.** Why? **"Comfortable people spend thousands of dollars; uncomfortable people tend to wait."** You must always remember this. I have been told that we must develop the ability to see through the lens of your customer. If you are sensing a theme here, you're right. Everything is dependent upon your confidence and your customer's comfort. Little things are important to your customers and everything either leads to a state of comfort or discomfort. And here is a key point to remember: the attempt to give the customer *everything* they want is not the goal, because, let's face it, you are not truly able to do this each and every time. You are obligated to make the customer believe that what we can give them or what we can do for them is, indeed, the best they can get and is everything they want. If you *always* strive to work in the customer's **interests or desires** and allow them to create a picture of Utopia in their own minds, an idea that cannot be realized, you will eventually create discomfort and a state of affairs that might make it impossible to deliver a vehicle to them. You must *lead* them to the sale, always utilizing our skills and positive energy – this book will show you how. *Guide* them into a comfortable frame of mind – again, this material will help you do this. If they understand, they will be comfortable. If they like our product more than another, they will buy it. If they do not prefer our product or if they do not understand our intentions and actions, they will not be comfortable and we will *not* sell them a car. Oh, by the way, we can certainly help them like our car more than others. In fact, we're kinda supposed to, aren't we? Are we going to run into the price-only customer from time to time, the one who cares nothing about experience or service? Yes, we will. And there will be ideas presented that will teach us how to take care of this type later. But remember, we do not usually lose deals because of dollars; we lose deals because we don't accomplish our primary goals – building comfort, value, and understanding.

Conceding to whim, or taking the path of least resistance will cost more money, short term and long term, than **being consistent and holding true to the system in place**. Now, I know this is difficult. Instant gratification is king. **Taking the path of least resistance is human nature and it takes strength to avoid following it**. Another factor is perceived failure or rejection. **Salespeople face these things potentially several times a day; not just once a week, or month, or quarter, or year, but all of the time.** We need to be strong and understand that activities will get us to our goals and that failure is never an option when our goals are based entirely in the tactics of the day. In other words... Do what we are supposed to do the same way every time and we can't lose.

Now a final thought before we move on... Sales has always been a sport as opposed to a science. If it were a science, then every salesperson could be assured of an exact same result for every action taken. This clearly is not the case because there are far too many variables involved. Further, if the same result could be expected by simply following a consistent procedure, everyone would do it. There would be no lack of confidence because there would be no rejection. However, because it is a sport, there are successes and failures. But one cannot base complete success or failure on a single made sale or a single lost sale. You are not a failure as a salesperson based on one lost sale - just as you are not a successful salesperson based on one tough close. Ultimately, our final career numbers are related to how much talent we had going in and how much we decided to work at our skill sets. Each *individual* opportunity is not always reflective of these things. In other words, if you handle everything properly and follow an effective procedure, it does not *guarantee* a favorable result. *However*, the results will be favorable far more often if this *is* done consistently.

OK. Got all that? Good.

Now, let's get down to business. .

What is the first opportunity to run into an obstacle or for a customer to become uncomfortable? Right!! The Welcome. And it's probably nothing that we do, is it? Well, maybe. But keep in mind that a customer is naturally uncomfortable when he/she steps out of the car at a dealership. The twinge of anxiety might come earlier. They might see some salespeople standing around waiting for them. I don't mean like some other dealerships: y'know, where all the salespeople are standing outside staring the customers down and waiting like a gauntlet for their victims to walk through. Not like that. What I mean is what can be seen through the fishbowl. An example would be just a group perhaps; a congregation, standing, or sitting. Don't have these huddles. They create discomfort. The customers get out of the car and they are already uncomfortable. Then, they are approached by a salesperson, and discomfort rises even more.

There are some training programs that promote the use of different words to describe things in our business a different way. I think that's a great idea, as long as we know that the words themselves don't get us where we want to be. Understand that you can use all the cute terminology you want to . . . Ours is a facility, not a dealership. We are consultants, not salespeople. Our people are guests, not customers. Whatever. Until our words and actions make the customer feel different; perhaps like they are in a *facility* and are being helped by a *consultant*, and are, in fact, our *guests*, it is all the same to them. It's our job to set the tone with a smile and a positive attitude and body language. No smile, bad energy, no posture – you are done before you get started. Before you find out whose customer they are or ascertain what they wish to accomplish, you must make it your only goal to make them comfortable at your store. Please believe me that nothing else matters at this point. Okay, enough of that.

Let's go over some basic Welcome word tracks. We'll use the formal welcome that most facilities would prefer to use. Much thought has been devoted to this, though, and, in our world, a genuine wave and hello is a very effective greeting if the other word tracks are included at some point. In fact, the ol' smile and wave should become a habit any time you see or pass a customer. Anyway. . .

Welcome Word Tracks

"Good Morning (afternoon, evening)! Welcome to Your Dealership. My name is Fred, and you are?"

This is pretty standard, but next you must begin to make them comfortable. Once more, be aware of your facial expression and in a nice genuine tone, you say. . .

"Pleasure to meet you. Thank you for choosing to spend some time with us today."

This does a couple of things. First, it should set them at ease a bit. But more, it basically tells them that we are grateful that they have decided to give some of their valuable time to us. Further, we are acknowledging that it is their choice to be here. What we have done is let the customer know that we believe they are important and intelligent. This goes a long way. Now we move into qualification. You ask . . .

"Well, _____, have you been here before? Perhaps purchased a vehicle (bought a car) here?"

Obviously, you ask these questions to jog the customer's memory a little, and to find out if they have recently worked with anyone else. Now, believe me, I'm a proponent of leaving such an impression on your customers that they immediately ask for you, but it is still courteous to find out when you can. Anyway, this book is not necessarily a complete Road to the Sale endeavor, so let's move on to the other important questions you must ask. And they are:

"What brings you in today? Were you referred by a friend or family member?"

These are important, particularly if you have a referral program in place. Chances are, a salesperson or consultant, whichever you prefer, will not enjoy paying his/her share if they do not deliver the unit. Let's help them out every chance we get. It's the right thing to do. Next.

"What would you like to accomplish today?"

And just a quick note, I have spoken to many others about asking two questions at once, an example being: "What brings you in today? Were you referred by a friend or family member?" Some believe it can be confusing, some don't really think it is. It's all about the delivery. I think it can be more conversation-natural and, as such, it should help the comfort level of our customers.

Keep in mind that a more formal welcoming is meant for those you *see* getting out of their car or walking into your showroom. If you greet someone you have not physically seen come from service or outside, a simple "have you been waited-on?" is extremely effective. Hearing the formal "Welcome" more than once will immediately become tiresome for your customer. You should always use a ten-foot rule and smile and say "hi" to anyone within that distance. Additionally, you might want to incorporate a ten-yard rule. It never hurts to smile and wave at a customer. It makes them feel good, and more comfortable.

We will talk about setting one another up for success as we progress here. What is meant by this is that a consultant should attempt to get all of the information his or her manager needs to properly assist with the deal. The manager, in turn, will provide everything the sales consultant needs to sell the vehicle and maximize gross profitability. There are two ideas to introduce that will be further probed next section: 1) Avoid speaking in specifics and absolutes whenever you are able (in short, don't offer up too much information) and 2) Tell the customers what they need to hear, not what they want to hear. Again, setting your manager up for success includes always preparing the customers – this includes making them as comfortable in your facility as possible. We don't want to have to backtrack on anything that has been said, so be careful.

Now, you've done your Welcome and you have properly qualified the customer (notice I did not say **pre-qualified**, which is the destructive practice of deciding in advance whether or not you have a buyer). Is the customer still uncomfortable? Probably. I don't want to *focus* on the 5%, but we should address it a bit. What if the customer does not wish to shake your hand or give you a name? It's okay. You just have work to do. If you simply smile, nod a nod of acknowledgement, and say "I understand. I think you will find it different here. I am at your service. What can I help you accomplish today?" you might find that they will lower their defenses more quickly than if you look put-off and react in a manner that is in the slightest bit irate. Whatever you do, don't take their reaction to you personally. Write this down. And then, write it down again. ***"Don't take anything personally."*** In fact, if you awake every morning and place yourself in such a state of mind, you will be happier and be more effective with your customers. If you greet someone and they are so defensive that they even seem to dislike you and you allow it to be personal, you might appear irritated. Imagine yourself and your reaction if you walk into a place of business and just want to be left alone a bit or just want to be made comfortable and the person who greets you becomes irritated because you are not gleefully acknowledging the desire to help you. Kind of a turn-off isn't it? And always keep in mind that a defensive posture is natural. Your customers might either be anxious or they may have been taught that this will help in the negotiation process.

Getting back to pre-qualification, I wanted to elaborate a bit for those of us new to this business. But, even the experienced among us remember having this bad habit cost us from time to time. And I'm sure we can remember how many times we said we would never do it again. Let's develop a picture, shall we? You're standing near the door with a couple of other consultants. It's already been decided that you are next to take a customer. You all spot a current-year vehicle driving through. You, pre-qualifying, remember the last couple of customers with current-year vehicles you have waited on. You did this only to find them owing a lot of money on that particular late model. Then you discovered the customer was trying to trade out of it and lower the monthly payment. Tough situation. And you believed it was a waste of time, not understanding that these people will not only buy another vehicle someday, when they can, but that they have a number of contacts represented by friends and family. So you graciously, nobly even, offer this opportunity to one of the other consultants standing with you. You don't think a lot of it; maybe walk away for a cup of coffee. A little later you notice the consultant still with the customers. They seem to have some rapport developed and look like they're having a bit of fun. You begin to feel a little sense of loss, a feeling that grows later when the other consultant is writing the people up without a trade-in. They needed another car. So when the vehicle is delivered, you initially might feel not only loss and regret, but you might find it in you to somehow rationalize that your friend on the sales floor owes you. Well, no. Get over it. Don't pre-qualify anyone. Don't assume someone cannot buy for any reason. You might not know the whole story.

Anyway, let's go over this again . . .

You go outside with a spring in your step; you're smiling brightly, and just glowing of confidence. You walk up to the customer who has just emerged from his/her car.

"Good Morning (Afternoon, Evening)! Welcome to Your Dealership. My name is Fred."

At this time, you may or may not wish to ask: "And you are. . ." Some suggest that you do, others feel it is intrusive (the belief being that you have not earned the right to ask the person their name). Please defer to your management for your tactic. My thoughts are that these folks must expect to be waited-on if they walk onto your lot or into your showroom during open hours. It follows that someone might ask them for their name. I don't think it is a bad thing. Again, rate, inflection, tone, and expression are always important no matter what you are saying. Be polite and courteous and calm. Anyway, what if you ask their name and they don't respond. And again, what if they ignore your attempt to shake their hand?

Remember, if someone is unresponsive, another way to counter is to simply continue with a portion of your Welcome word track. You say: *"Well, thank you for choosing to spend some time with us today,"* and smile. Continue: *"Please make yourself at home. What can I help you accomplish today?"*

Now, as tempting as it is to try to empathize here (and there is a place for empathy) and say something to the effect of "I see. You've probably had a bad experience at another dealership or you were treated poorly is the past, but I can tell you . . ." Hold it right there. While this might be true, you do not necessarily want to bring up or out any other negative emotions at this point. You also risk sounding a bit arrogant in assuming that this was their reasoning behind their initial defense. In reality, there may be any number of reasons a person might be unreceptive, maybe having nothing to do with past car buying experiences. Leave any type of psycho-analysis to the experts. Or even more fun, you and your manager can take stabs at it after your customer leaves you, hopefully after having taken delivery. But let us stick to the basics. And here's something that should be part of the basics...

Warm Fuzzies

I'm not absolutely certain when the term "warm fuzzies" was coined. It refers to words said at certain times, in certain ways that impart exactly that feeling to your customers. These warm fuzzies are one of the major ways to shorten a *customer's shopping list*, which we'll talk about near the end of this chapter. We want to make sure that we toss these in whenever the level of comfort seems to be waning a bit. Here are some examples of warm fuzzies:

1. **I'm/We're grateful.**
2. **I'm/We're at your service.**
3. **Please forgive me/us.**
4. **You're very important to us.**
5. **I'm here for you.**
6. **We want you to be very comfortable here.**
7. **Please come in and say "hi." You're always welcome here.**

These are just a sampling, but feel free to create your own. Obviously, delivery is important too. We don't want to be ridiculously over the top or blatantly fawning over these people. That would put a dent in the trust level and take the customer comfort the opposite direction. These, as with all other words, should be practiced frequently, if not daily. It doesn't hurt to be courteous to fellow employees either – might put you in the mood to do the same for your customers if you're having a particularly off-day.

Warm fuzzies will also be used in conjunction with counters and/or closing questions or statements, so look for them. This being said, I have had cases where sales consultants or managers believe these things to be a little too warm and fuzzy, particularly in a closing situation. I, of course, would ask them how. How could something meant to melt the customer's heart be detrimental to the closing of a car deal? Well, sometimes, I was told, you have to give it to people straight. Sometimes, a certain personality will not gel with "nice." I get it. What I told these people is that it doesn't matter what the personality might be, we will always be direct when closing and negotiating. It doesn't mean we can't be respectful and courteous. The warm fuzzies simply soften up the situation, and they do it well. As we move forward into the countering concerns and objections sections, you will see how to hit, pull-back or retreat, then do it again. Oh, wait... We've already introduced the Technique. Moving on...

Okay, let's get back to the welcome . . . you've just asked the customer what you can help them accomplish and look out! Here it comes!! The dreaded "Just looking!!"

We have spoken about a change in mind-set. Now is the time to use it. I can remember how devastating it was to hear "Just looking" early in my career. This was because no one explained to me exactly what this means. All I thought I knew was that these people were not going to buy a car today, and what was more, they probably wanted me to leave them alone. Talk about pressure. I was pleading in my mind "Please don't leave me," or "Please don't ask to be left alone." Number one, I had no clue how to regain control of the situation (not poor training, but no training); number two, I would most assuredly be grilled by my manager and fellow salespeople as to why I *dusted* this *up*. Yeah, were just chock-full of all kinds of neat terminology in this business, aren't we?

So what does it mean when a customer says "just looking?" Well, it's just a **conditioned response**. What it means is "Please let me catch my breath and allow me to get comfortable." Mind-set change – Go against the previous things you have heard on this subject and **hope** you get a "just looking' response. I have heard strategies that teach a consultant how to avoid this "objection." They don't work. People will find a way to respond with "Just lookin'" no matter how you start the conversation. Have you ever asked someone if it's wonderful weather you're having and had them respond with "just looking?" How about "How are you doing today?" or "Are you looking for new or used?" You got it. "Just lookin'" And what is more, it is not a true objection. Understand this...You have more opportunity to sell a vehicle today to someone who says "just looking" than you do to someone who pops out of their trade-in, points to a new vehicle and says "I want to buy that car." Do you believe this to be true? Does it make sense? Well, why? Let me ask you . . . What do you have to discuss with this customer other than price and/or trade-in value? You're right. Nothing. You have no rapport. Have you been able to build comfort, value, or understanding? Of course not. If someone says "just looking" your already bright face should light up even more. You actually have the opportunity to sell a vehicle, and yourself, and the dealership. How about that? So a customer tells you they are "just looking." What do you say? Well, you don't say what you've might have said in the past, or perhaps what your competition might say. Things like: What are you looking for? Did you have anything in particular in mind? None of these are really effective. I think you can understand why. It's because you have just intruded with another question.

Here's is what we should do. **Cheerfully begin assisting them right away**. Give them a lay of the land, so to speak. This must be valuable, since they are, of course, just looking. Begin with a positive statement: "We're just looking." "Great! Wonderful! Fantastic!" The key here is to be sincere. Use one of your Welcome word tracks, "Well, thank you for choosing to spend some time with us today." Then go into this: "As you look around, you will find all of our pre-owned (premium certified and certified included) on the front perimeter (show them with gestures). Over there you will see our fine selection of compact cars, both 3-doors and 5-doors. And beside them will be our newly redesigned compact sport utility. Our flagship vehicle, the _____, probably the best value in a mid-sized sedan in two decades, is there. And the revolutionary crossover, the _____, is in that area. If you are here to see the state-of-the-art _____ . . ." You get the picture. The actual descriptiveness is at your discretion, but try to jazz it up a little. If you are an independent used vehicle facility, focus on the various makes and models you have in inventory.

Now you will want to use a staple in sales, a bridge and an either/or. "Now that you are a bit familiar with our display (the bridge), are you looking more for new or pre-owned (the either/or)?" If you do this each and every time, you will find that the interview process begins to flow naturally for you more often than not. Are there people who are mad at the world and who will flat tell you to leave them alone? Yep. You bet. This doesn't happen often, but when it does, give in and say the following: "Please make yourselves at home. We're here for you whenever you're ready. I just didn't want you to think you were being ignored." If still nothing comes of this, let them be and inform your manager. **The difference between the untrained and a true professional is that the professional will try and try again before they give up, and only at the point where they are sensing that anything more will create discomfort in the customer.**

Some will really push the limit. I recall one of my colleagues stating that if we don't lose one now and again, we're not trying hard enough. They recognize the rejection as opportunity. It's a professional mind-set as opposed to an untrained mind-set. But as for the prior philosophy, I believe that you don't ever really have to lose one if your skills are strong and your positive attitude shines through. Utopia? Ah, maybe. But what the heck... Believe it and live it.

Another tactic was one that was brought up at a Manager's workshop I attended some years back. One of the managers mentioned that someone had taught him to begin to walk away and then turn and say "Oh, and if you have any questions, I'll be right over here." Sounds simple enough, and many of us have heard this idea before, but maybe not with the accentuated turn. He said that it was the turn that actually made people respond. More often than not, they will have a question at this point and you can begin your interview or investigation. It has been since named the **Columbo**, after the famous television detective who mercilessly tormented criminals into cracking. Obviously, we are not into merciless torment, but we would like another shot to break the ice. Anyway, the whole purpose, the initial goal is to make these people a legitimate contact. Find a way to get their information: name, address, and phone number. It is simply not good enough to answer a couple of questions, maybe give them a brochure and a business card and have them say "thank you" and leave. Offer them competitive comparison information if nothing else. Get them to your desk and get their information. It's the one of the first ways to build loyalty. When they do return, the chances of asking for you have been greatly increased. Another very important thing is that these people are now contacts, and they have friends and family. Try something like this. "Before you go, let me give you some more information, perhaps a comparison, that will help you make your decision." And then walk toward your desk. We will talk more about "Before you go" later. Now, it might *sound* very strange to use the words "Before you go," but those words are even more useful during a turn-over or closing attempt.

The next most likely spot for an objection of sorts to pop up would be during a presentation, or perhaps even before, when the customer decides to look at a car before *you* decide to show it. Has this ever happened to you? And what would this be? Well, it's the most obvious. Most of us have it clearly marked on every vehicle. If we don't, we'll certainly throw something out there. You guessed it – Price. But, we must cover something else first, after we re-cap this chapter.

We've learned a lot in this chapter.

Chapter In-Review

1. **We discussed how important it is to *get into character* and stay in it.**

This is not always an easy thing, but it's necessary. We know we're human beings and we're going to have bad days. We just can't have them in front of the customer. I have heard the idea that we should come to work and just leave our troubles on the curb outside in an imaginary paper sack, then pick it up on the way out. I've got a better idea... Acknowledge your troubles. The last thing you want is to have them pop up on you when you least expect it, taking you out of character at the worst time.

2. "Comfortable people spend thousands of dollars; uncomfortable people tend to wait."

Smile and wave. Do everything you can to make your people feel good about being at the dealership and being in your hands. Warm fuzzies and courtesy go a long way. Keep these things a focus. Also, be aware of your surroundings. You never know who might be able to see or hear you.

3. Avoid pre-qualification

Stay aggressive with respect to waiting on guests. Give them their space, but do not jump to bad conclusions about their ability to buy or wants, need, or desires. Do your job – make them love you and sell them a car.

4. We talked about "Just looking" and the Columbo.

We chose a mind-set change rather than discouragement. Practice the skills and word tracks that will get us past the "just looking" stage and into the needs assessment or interview. Do it all of the time and your results will be clear.

5. Customer's shopping list

We mentioned that shortening the customer's list is something that can be accomplished through comfort levels and with the help of warm fuzzies. Let's be clear... The ultimate goal is to eliminate the shopping list and have them buy the vehicle from us now. How? We have to focus on the customer's experience and make it the best they've ever had. Your presentation must be world-class. *Become a dinner topic.* If your customer does not purchase on that day, make certain they are going to talk about you and how wonderfully they were treated. This will certainly go a long way toward keeping them in the store or not wanting to visit another facility.

BEYOND THE WALKAROUND

Preparing For Purchase Consultation

There are a number of things we can do to make sure we are fully prepared when it comes time to talk price. Keep in mind that many of your customers have been trained or advised to not appear to want the vehicle as much as they might, certainly not to show urgency of any kind. But some are actually surly in their negativity – though thankfully, not a high percentage. Our job, and we'll learn more about this when Feigned Indifference is introduced, is to not allow any of this to alter how we build the customer's comfort level and keep our confidence at its highest also. There are a few things that will help us with this.

Customer Comfort and Consultant Confidence

I wanted to revisit these ideas for a bit before we move forward. I have made it clear how important these are to our everyday success, but how are they truly related and how can we be sure we do everything we can to maintain them? This is how we must prioritize every day. I wanted to simplify life many years ago, professional life that is, so I made everything about this. Customer Comfort and Consultant Confidence are directly proportional (at what percentage I do not know – remember formulas that don't make sense?) which means as one rises, so does the other; when one falls, the other does as well. An example of this is seen when a consultant does happen to greet one of the surly types. One can almost see the confidence leaking out. Why? Well, the consultant does not see how he or she will be able to make any progress, let alone a car deal, with this grouchy person. The customer has a low comfort level and is bringing the sales consultant down with them. The key is for the professional to have so much knowledge, skill, and confidence that he/she is able to break through the exterior of the customer and make them feel more at ease. We can do this almost every time, but we have to study, learn, and practice. Once the confidence level is high, it has a tendency to stay there. The ability to counter concerns and objections is what creates success and confidence with staying power. Now, back to the directly proportional thing and how vital it all is. To simplify, if we do something that decreases the comfort level of a customer or the confidence level of an employee, we've probably done the wrong thing. It is the same with the words we say. If we lower these things, we've probably said the wrong thing. So, be careful and stay positive.

Needs Assessment and Interview

Although this is a very important part of preparing us to counter any price concerns and help us set ourselves up for success, we are not going to dive into the nuts and bolts. But, we are going to describe the basics and provide an introduction of sorts. All facilities should have a set of solid interview questions for the consultants. Almost all training programs will spend a good amount of time on this subject also. Part of getting better is to read or listen to all available material, and there is a lot of good stuff out there. What I will do is provide a list of questions we should be able to answer about our customers. It will be at the end of this chapter. Now, as far as gathering information from your guests that is important for placing them on the correct vehicle, it generally begins after the "What would you like to accomplish today?"

This will get you to a starting point, more often than not. And this starting point can be as perfect as the customer wanting to tell you needs and desires up front and then leading to a great presentation (textbook road to the sale), or it can be "Gimme yer best price on an Accord!" How we handle the latter will be a subject in the very near future. The former, though, or anything similar to that, will open up the next step with this, almost as an aside while moving toward your desk.

"So what piqued (if you prefer not to use "piqued," I get it – go with something similar) your interest in the Accord, John? Did you see one on the road and were attracted by its look or does someone you know own one?"

If we are unable to get off price, we can then follow with *Positive Value Statements* or *Pre-emptive Strikes*.

PRE-EMPTIVE STRIKE:

"A surprise attack that is launched in order to prevent the enemy (adversary) from doing it to you."

I have had discussions about the term "pre-emptive strike." Some have commented that selling a vehicle is ultimately a partnership between consultant and customer. It should never be adversarial, nor should the customer be thought of as an enemy. These same individuals were also a bit surprised that someone as committed to customer comfort and the utilization of "warm fuzzies" as I am would use such a term. After all, I am a proponent of making people feel good about everything at the dealership. Yes, but... Make no mistake, we are going head to head almost every time we work with a customer. Not necessarily against the customer themselves, but against misconceptions, bad information, false perceptions, etc. and you name it. Utilizing positive value statements, pre-emptive strikes, and consistently countering is how we ultimately create an ally.

POSITIVE VALUE STATEMENTS

Building Value (Strategy)

Statements (Tactics)

1. "Our manufacturer's value pricing helps keep all of the advancements in safety and technology affordable (a great benefit) for nearly everyone."
2. "These vehicles are simply the best value of any vehicles, anywhere!"
3. "These vehicles represent a fantastic value at list price, let alone with the benefit of any incentives."
4. "Our elite service team has saved many of my customers hundreds of dollars on dozens of occasions!"
   a. By having the car fixed right the first time (time=$).

   b. By providing helpful consultation to **prevent** costly repairs.

5. "The manufacturer's aggressive incentives have virtually removed the need for negotiation."
6. "Other markets or facilities are simply not interested in selling vehicles at the price we are able to provide!"
7. "We spend more of our money to ensure you save more of yours." (Relates to pre-owned)

At any rate, we would then like to move back into the **Interview or Needs Assessment**. Again, be sure to check the list of questions at the end of the chapter.

This needn't be an interrogation. In fact, if the customer feels such is becoming the case, the comfort level will drop quickly and you will have little opportunity to get it back. Here are a few keys to success...

1. Allow the customer to respond and you LISTEN.

2. Do not talk about yourself.

3. Smile and ask questions with genuine care and interest.

A quick side-note here... When you are listening to your customers, please learn to **"hang on their every word."** This was something that endeared many people to Thomas Jefferson. Jon Meacham's Thomas Jefferson: The Art of Power is a fantastic biography which really teaches us some great ideas with respect to dealing with others. Not that Jefferson was loved by all – far from it – but he did have amazing qualities which allowed him to influence many. Meacham made Jefferson come to life and we could actually visualize the man waiting on every word of his guests with such anticipation as that word might be the most relevant ever uttered by a human being. Think about how important the speaker must have felt. Use this to *show* people how important they are rather then *telling* them so.

Now, let's go over the necessary information you must try to secure prior to quoting numbers of any kind (yes, this includes any published prices or specials!).

VEHICLE

We need to make certain that we are on the correct vehicle - the color, equipment, all the hot buttons. Follow any acronym you have been taught, ex. SPACED – Safety, Performance, Comfort and Convenience, Economy, Dependability. Provide the customer with a world-class presentation and have them *drive* the vehicle they wish to own.

It is also not a bad thing to ask the customer if they are considering other options. If it's me, I'd want to know what I'm up against early. This way, most presentations can be tailored to this and be far more effective.

BUDGET

True, we are not financial consultants. But, if we are able to learn a true idea of budget and WHY the customer must stay within this, we will be in a better place to be sure. Now, the budget can have a total dollar goal or a payment goal. Be careful that they are not the same and the customer simply has a misconception about how this translates to payment. For now, it's enough for you to know that if you go to the sales desk with the statement that the customer has to be under $20,000 and you are asked "Why?" you should know. Is it truly total dollars? Did the customer's bank tell them that 20K was all that they qualified for? Does this figure represent a payment? What terms would those be and who quoted them? Drill down. It will help you counter concerns.

TRADE-IN

Yes, I know that a percentage of our customers are trained or coached to withhold the trade until a price has been secured. We need to overcome this whenever possible. Find out if there is a trade and a pay-off. Ah, the pay-off. What if the customer does not wish to divulge this either? Appeal to the fact that you are only here to be of service and that the customer is under no obligation to buy. And since there is no relationship between what is owed and what the vehicle is worth, there is no point is keeping the information to oneself. In fact, it is required to quote a payment.

Asking for expectations with respect to trade-in value was, and still is, frowned upon by some. The reasoning is that if the customer throws out a number and nothing is said until the appraisal, there is the assumption that the value can be met. I'd rather know and counter this early.   We will be able to do this very skillfully after studying and learning the Trade-In chapter.

TIME-FRAME

Leading into a trial-close opportunity, and understanding that no matter what the answer, you must still ask for the business multiple times, getting a time-frame out of your customer is a necessity. If the customer says "Why would you ask?" or "Why do you need to know?" you respond with the following:

"John, it is just for your benefit. Our incentives do change and some are diminishing assets. I want to make sure you have accurate information."

This should certainly warrant a response, an "I understand" or a "What do you mean?" As with all counters, the "I understand" is the goal. A "What do you mean?" opens up a dialogue, during which we will build value and/or justify our dollars or position. And, with respect to diminishing assets, we are referring to a certificate or cash that is not tied to a particular program and might run out.

Moving on to the **trial-close**...

"John, if we can work this out from a financial standpoint, and I'm sure we will, is this something you would like to do today?"

This is so simple, easy, straight-forward, and non-confrontational. This does not have to be done after the return from the demonstration, though, in a perfect world, that would be wonderful. Likewise, if we jump directly to numbers because we receive a thumbs-up to this statement prior to our building of value and the driving of the unit, we are shooting ourselves in the foot.

Trial closes can be used at almost any time should the situation call for one. An example would be that the customer demands your best price on the vehicle before you have a chance to do a needs assessment, presentation, or demonstration. So, what to do with the "Gimme yer best price!" guy? Try this...

"John, I will gladly give you a wonderful price on this vehicle, provided it is one you would like to own (Price Counter). How did you become interested in the Accord? Did you see one on the road or does a friend own one?" (Transition to Needs Assessment)

Hopefully, this will begin the Interview for you. If not... "My buddy has one. Just gimme yer best price!"

"Of course, we won't lose a deal (your business) over dollars (Price Counter). In fact, understanding that we all pay the same for these vehicles, is this something you would like to do today if it all works out from a budget standpoint? "(Transition to Trial Close)

We have just used a couple of statements we will learn here in just a bit. But first...

Before we address price directly, let's talk about philosophy for a while. Now I don't mean the rational investigation of the truths and principles of being, knowledge, or conduct, but our philosophy - our pricing philosophy to be more specific. What it is, what it means, and how we make our customers understand it.

We have the factory window sticker placed on every new vehicle in stock, as well as any addendum that has been added. If we are not a one-price store, we will negotiate at the right time and if need be. This is how we choose to do business. If we are a one-price facility, we will likely have that price broken down with discounts and incentives on some type of hang-tag. If we have our pre-owned or used car prices posted or whether we will quote them as the situation seems to dictate, we will handle our positive statements the very same way. And whether or not we work a traditional four-square or a modified four-square or some other system is entirely up to your facility. What it means is that your management staff will evaluate the situation, looking at a number of different things: availability, age, rate of sale, and/or other factors to discern exactly what it will take to move a particular unit. Your job, as a salesperson, is to help them by establishing certain positive emotions and confidences in your customers that will enable them and you to hold the highest gross profit attainable on *every*, let me make this clear, *every* unit. To begin, we should try to stay off price specifically, but build the comfort level of our customer to its highest level.

For negotiation stores we are going to learn five statements that will be invaluable to us. A few one-price statements will follow. These are more positive value statements that can be used throughout the presentation. They will be our foundation. They will, depending upon delivery and our ability not to take anything personally, allow us to build the comfort and confidence in our customer, and, most importantly produce a presentation to allow us to create a high level of value versus price. And, even more vital, these statements will help us to avoid saying the word "no," in this case "no" meaning "I won't give you a price." They also help us stay off of price altogether and build value as well. Now, please understand that no one is foolish enough to believe that these statements and any subsequent word tracks or ideas in this program are cure-all, end-alls. It has been noted just how difficult our job can be and how tough to deal with certain customers might be. Everything presented here is designed to help sell as many vehicles as possible and save every dollar of gross that we can, all the time, every time. Enough on that for now. And now I'll mention it again, our primary goal is to have the customer respond with either an "I understand," after which you may attempt to close the sale itself or the particular step on the road to the sale that might be next, or a "What do you mean?" that will enable you to respond further, perhaps with the use of a third party example. Here are the statements for those of us who choose to negotiate:

1. We have found that this particular vehicle, with this equipment, has been selling very well for very close to this figure.

2. We will not lose a deal over dollars. Your referrals and repeat business are very important to us.

3. We will happily provide you with a wonderful price for this unit. Let us make certain that is the one you would like to own.

4. At Our Dealership, we make it simple and easy for everyone, and you always get more than what you pay for!"

And an additional option for new car facilities...

5. "Please keep in mind that the great incentives and reduced profit margins are designed to keep the selling price at or very close to MSRP, particularly on this model that has become a customer favorite here."

You must commit these to memory and learn them backwards and forwards. And you will. Here are a few for One-Price stores (note that a couple of the prior statements will work also)...

1. We provide a no-hassle, no-haggle environment.

2. **We chose a culture that does not include negotiation.**

3. **We prefer to relate to our guests with integrity.**

4. **At Our Dealership, we make it simple and easy for everyone, and you always get more than what you pay for!"**

And what I mean by backwards and forwards is that you are able to recite them by number. They are numbered, so attach that to each of them. Write them, again numbered, on index cards (old-fashioned, but effective). It might seem silly to some, but it really does help with memory.

Why are these so important? Well, what if your customer is, indeed, unfamiliar with your dealership and they have questions or concerns?

"Can you gimme your best price" or "Can you tell me what the best you can do is?"

"I would be happy to provide you with a wonderful price for this unit (vehicle). Please let us make certain it is the one you would like to own."

Or, if a One-Price store:

"We are a no-hassle, no-haggle environment."

"Can you tell me how much will you discount this vehicle?"

"We have found that this particular vehicle, with this equipment has been selling very well for very close to this figure."

Again, for a non-negotiation selling philosophy:

"We chose a culture that does not include negotiation."

"The other _____ store in _____ city will knock $3,000 off their cars. Will you?"

"We won't lose a deal over dollars. Your referrals and repeat business are very important to us."

One-Price... And remember that these just allow you to get to the next step sometimes. You will have to be able to justify your philosophy further if the opportunity comes up. This is what we want.

"We have posted our one-low price which includes discounts and incentives. If you qualify for more, you will certainly get them all. We prefer to relate to our guests with integrity."

"Can you tell me why should I buy from you?"

"For a lot of reasons. But mainly, because at Our Dealership it's simple and easy for everyone, and you always get more than what you pay for!"

Do you see how these work?

Here is the beauty of this. Not once have you said the word "no" nor have you given the customer a definite number or even an idea. Again, there are times that you must, but there are sound tactics that will prevent it almost all of the time. Get good at this and you will close more deals. You can also use variations of these statements, perhaps in reverse. The customer asks if you can just take a little off (I love this one. They don't tell you how much would be enough for them) and you can respond immediately:

"Were this a vehicle not selling very well for very close to this figure, maybe a little more, it would be a simple matter. But please rest assured that it is worth every dollar and more at this price."

This is designed to save you not only the deal, but valuable gross profit. Since, of course, your manager will probably take a lesser dollar, your job is to minimize that amount during any negotiation process. These statements are designed to do just this. These can also work well when competing with advertisements from other dealerships. Obviously, ridiculously reduced loss-leaders are advertised to lure out-of-town business. We will address these in even more detail next section. Now, earlier I mentioned that some customers simply do not get it, or don't want to. There are going to be cases when you cannot meet the expectations of the customer, or make them understand what you are saying or doing. If this

were not the case, we'd sell everyone on the spot –
sometimes it takes a little longer... A case in point was the
time a young couple had been the recipient of some
misinformation on the internet. Imagine that! They were
looking to purchase two new vehicles. In some major
breakdown in communication and process, they came in
with a check from their credit union that covered
everything but taxes (we'll talk about how to avoid this in
the payments section). We had already done all we could
to put the two-car deal together – all-in on all avenues.
They still felt the trades were hit too low and that we
should be able to cover the difference in taxes. Well, we
used all of the word tracks and third-party examples we
could, but it ultimately came down to the idea that we
expressed at the end. *It would be extremely bad business
for us to come in to work every day and not do everything
we could to sell a single car, let alone two.* And we have, I
said. The couple left, leaving both new vehicles behind.
They reconsidered the next day and took both. Yes, there
will be times when all of the material you will learn here
just won't work. But, you will pick up several more deals
because of your skill and consistency. This stuff is
powerful, but you must believe in it. If there are thoughts
out there about how this information seems to lend itself
to reason rather than emotion, and that sales is mostly
emotional, those thoughts are accurate. Keep in mind that
***we must attempt to keep the positive emotional
connection, but also break through the negative with
logic and reason. Once this is done, once we have
created that little crack in the emotional defense, our
closing potential is greatly increased.***

Will this compassionate bid for the customer's
comfort be successful 100% of the time? Of course not.

But, having these skills and utilizing them will put us way ahead of the game. And next section we will go over quite a few more. The very last thing we want to do is to look surprised somehow or be caught off-guard. You can call it the old deer in the headlights look, or way better than that, an outstanding trainer named Tim Porter likened the look to an Amish farmer at Best Buy. I suppose it's not 100% politically correct, and I'll apologize to any of our Amish salespeople, but . . . That one cracks me up every time I hear it, and Tim's ability to take on that look in class is priceless, if you can imagine. Anyway, if you cannot respond quickly and intelligently to a customer's concern you will lose credibility fast and they will become uncomfortable with you. Timing is everything. **You _must_ counter immediately, intelligently, and confidently.** You can't do one of these: "Hey John, remember when you asked me what my best price was a while ago and I stuttered and really didn't have an answer. Well I had something else on my mind. Anyhow, what I meant to say was that we would happily provide you with a wonderful price on this unit, if it is, in fact, one you would like to own. You okay now. Does that make sense? Okay great." Uh-uh. Not good. Your response must be immediate. You will come off as professional and the trust and comfort level will grow.

Now, since we are here, let's work with some specifics. It would be doing everyone an injustice by telling you what you must do without showing you how. You will always have something effective to say. Later, we'll go over some key responses and practice them. Most of these are interchangeable between new and used vehicles, but some work better with one or the other. Again, the secret is to always have something intelligent to say *right now*. A simple, matter-of-fact response that makes sense will improve your customer's comfort level enormously.

It is interesting to note that depending upon when these statements are used in the process, and they may be used anytime, you might be able to set up a close. I will explain setting up a close and then following with a closing question.

It works like this: a customer is involved in the negotiation, he then works you for a better deal...

"All right, you knock five hundred off and we've got a deal."

"Remember I mentioned that this vehicle, with this equipment has been selling very well for very close to this figure? Understanding this, shall we continue with the paperwork?

Once you have these committed to memory, you will be able to follow them with closing statements and questions. The first of these, the easiest and perhaps least confrontational, was developed because many salespeople seemed to have difficulty asking for the business. The old "Would you like to own this today?" or the terribly weak "How does this sound or seem to you?" just wasn't cutting it for them. In fact, it seemed some salespeople were waiting for the *customer* to *ask* them to *sell* the car. I wanted to give those salespeople something simple that would make them more at ease when asking the "big question." I am sure you have heard these before in one form or another, and here they are:

1. "Shall we (Why don't we, Let's) continue with the paperwork?"

2. "Shall we continue with the process?"

3. "Shall I put your name on the vehicle then?"

4. "How will you be registering your vehicle today?"

5. "Will you title this vehicle in one name or both?"

6. "Can you pick the vehicle up (take delivery of your car) at 4:15 or would 4:45 be better?"

7. "Shall I have the vehicle cleaned-up for immediate delivery if possible?"

8. "Shall I have the Paint Protectant applied today before you take delivery or would you prefer to take your new car now and bring it back next week?"

Anything like these will work nicely if used firmly and at the proper time. Number One can be used almost all of the time. The customer will understand that you are asking them to buy the unit. Even a simple, "Shall we continue?" might suffice. And, Number Two "Shall we continue with the process?" is ideal when closing on a particular step on the road to the sale.

For other purposes, it is fitting to acknowledge that we are closing whenever we wish to move to another step in the Road To The Sale. You can use these, not necessarily to close the sale but to close to a presentation or demonstration drive.

Ex: The customer asks if you'll take $500 or more off the price of the vehicle before he/she has been given a presentation. The salesperson responds:

"Incentives, including high rebates or low interest rates, along with reduced profit margins have made this unit a customer favorite at our store. Considering this, shall we take a closer look at the vehicle?"

Go on and show the unit until they come up with another concern, then follow the same procedure.

Now here is another way to counter a concern about our pricing...

"Can you tell me your best price on this used vehicle?"

"This vehicle is priced nicely, and we will be happy to provide you with a wonderful bottom line for this unit, if it is, in fact, one you would like to own. I would like to make sure this would be a great fit for you. Keeping this in mind, shall we take a closer look at the vehicle?"

The customer might ask the questions in similar forms or inflections, but the essence is the same. The goal here, as in most situations is to make our point without the customer losing face or comfort level. Depending on the customer, we might not be able to avoid this. But, with practice, your delivery of the message should itself become comforting. Pick and choose the proper responses from those given in this session. Practice them and you will be able to work them like an artist. Just remember to close. Don't wait for the customer to ask you. Again, we are looking at some countering word tracks here, and we are dabbling with transitional phrases and closing questions. All of these will be put together when The Technique is presented in a short while.

Chapter In-Review

1. Customer Comfort and Consultant Confidence

We pointed out that these factors are directly proportional and directly tied to one another. This is a common theme and one to always have in mind when we take action or speak. With respect to our fellow consultants, it's our responsibility to also raise their levels of confidence rather than cut it down.

2. Pre-Emptive Strikes and Positive Value Statements

These tactics are extremely important during the early stages in particular. Anything we can do to build value in ourselves and our product will make the road to the sale quite a bit smoother. It is easier and more effective to beat the customer to the punch, so to speak, and counter any lack of urgency or attempted devaluation before it happens.

3. Need Assessment/Trial Close

While we did not dive into these things fully, the importance was made clear. Put these customers on the right vehicle and find out if they are ready to buy. It's okay if they are not, and we will discover how to create a bit more urgency in all of our customers in just a short while.

4. Closing Questions and How To Close From Counters

We just scratched the surface on these. There are a lot more to come. We talked about how we are closing all the time, mostly from one step of the sale to the next. If the customer does not wish us to show the car, we have to close them on the presentation. If they do not wish to drive the unit, we must close on the demonstration, and so forth.

BASIC INTERVIEW/NEEDS ASSESSMENT QUESTIONS

- Have they been here before?
- Have you been referred here by a friend or family member?
- Have they purchased a vehicle here before?
- What kind of vehicle are they driving now?
- What do they like about it that they would like in their next vehicle?
- What would they like to change most about their current vehicle?
- What else would they like in their next vehicle?
- Who's the vehicle for?
- Will it be for business or personal use?
- Is gas mileage a concern?
- Will they prefer a larger or smaller vehicle?

- Do they like lighter or darker colors?
- What brought them to our store?
- What other models are they considering?
- Is cargo space important?
- Do they have a job?
- Do they have full coverage insurance?
- Do they have a valid driver's license?
- Do they prefer to pay cash, lease, or finance?
- Are they familiar with our philosophy (One-Price or other Pricing Philosophy)?
- Are there other decision makers involved?
- Have they done research on the vehicle they're looking at?
- Have they done research on their trade?
- Do they have a payoff?
- What is their current payment?
- Who is their bank or credit union?
- When do they plan to make a decision?
- Do they need to trade in order to buy our car?
- What is their e-mail address?
- Where do they work?
- What do they do for a living?
- Do they understand value vs. price?
- When can you contact them again (if they are leaving)?
- Are they comfortable here?
- Is there a different feeling for them here than they have had at other dealerships?
- Where are they from?
- What is it they would like to accomplish today?

BEYOND THE WALKAROUND

Feigned Indifference and the Technique

FEIGNED INDIFFERENCE

As stated before, the single most important concept within the material of "Beyond the Walkaround" might very well be Feigned Indifference.

The word "feign" means to put on an appearance of or to make believe or pretend.

"Indifference" means without interest or concern or having no bias or preference.

And so Feigned Indifference, as defined as a concept in a sales philosophy and in this case the car business, would be *to put on the appearance of having no bias or preference with regard to the sale of a vehicle*. In other words, you *act* as though you do not *need* to sell this vehicle now. The idea, of course, is to do this and at the same time make the customer believe that you would indeed love to have their business at some point. Just as in a purchase situation, a *need* is different than a *want*. *Needing* to sell the vehicle now develops an air of desperation and pressure. Merely *wanting* to sell the car will allow for the care and empathy to come through leading to customer comfort. Think back to the secret of the car business: Keep the consultants (employees) confident and the customers comfortable. This being said, it is, of course, still our objective to sell and deliver every customer a vehicle as soon as possible. Remember, the indifference is *feigned*.

The attitude represented by Feigned Indifference will make your words far more powerful, because defenses are naturally dropped. Remember, "Before you go?" "Before you go" is an example of Feigned Indifference. In the mind of the customer, they have achieved what they have wanted – they're gone. You have released them. But, just because you have done this, it does not mean that you stop selling or stop trying to close. You continue and ask for the sale yet again.

Okay, we've discovered what Feigned Indifference is, but how do you get it? More importantly, how do you keep it? First, it must be understood that this attribute originates in only three ways: It is either present from birth (a natural talent), discovered by accident, or developed through awareness and training.

Very rare is the individual born with this attribute. And even rarer might be finding such a person in auto sales where ultra-enthusiasm and aggressiveness are taught. But occasionally, someone comes along. Allow me to briefly relate to you the story of Leonard Schmidt. Leonard had had his position at a factory eliminated and was diligently seeking new employment when he applied

for a position at our store some years ago. The first
interview had us believing that he was a very nice fellow,
but one who might not take rejection particularly well.
Leonard was of middle age with light thinning hair,
perhaps six foot five and a bit lanky, and always seemed to
have an expression of happiness. So even with his height
there was certainly no intimidating presence about him.
Leonard was relatively quiet and pleasant. To make a long
story short, we did interview him again and we found him
so darn likeable, we hired him. Now likeability is
important, but it's generally not enough on its own. It
really was for Leonard. Anyway, after a couple of weeks of
initial sales training, Leonard was scheduled in and began
waiting on customers. In his first two months, Leonard
outsold salespeople who had been at the store 7 and 10
years. Could have been beginners luck. I've seen it
throughout my career. But, as might be the case in your
store, it takes time for repeat and referral business to kick
in. Leonard didn't need it. He was still the same old
Leonard, but he suddenly showed a confidence that
somehow had not been present during the interview
process. Then we began listening to him and watching him
more closely with his customers. It seemed as though he
was never fazed by anything the people said to him. He
took nothing personally and always tried to put his
customers at ease. It was as though he had a natural
ability to make people believe he was absolutely no threat
to them or their hard-earned money. It was as if it made
little difference to him whether someone bought a vehicle
or not. He acted like he was there to provide a service for
them: help them with information, give options, and
generally just make life easy. If the customers chose to
buy a vehicle, wonderful! If not, well, they were in control
(so they thought) and it was always their decision. Don't

misunderstand, Leonard wanted to sell everyone he met a vehicle and he needed the money. But, it just never really came across that way to his customer. And Leonard *always* asked for the business. Leonard was feigned indifference personified.

The second way mentioned as to how one might acquire this trait is to discover the attribute by accident and then, understanding how valuable it is, to continue to use it always. Here are a couple of examples of how a consultant may enter a particular state that allows for a bit of indifference.

The first is that the salesperson has the month made early. What I mean by this is that a salesperson got off to an awesome start and has surpassed his/her unit and monetary goals with substantial time left in the month. Does this mean the salesperson will now fold up and do nothing? On the contrary, this salesperson has just a bit of indifference creep into the persona. A customer says they are buying in a year, or they didn't get enough for their trade, or the price is too high, whatever. This salesperson is still smiling, not taking the concern or objection personally, and simply tries to help the customer out. If that customer does not buy, it is not the end of the world. There is no being under pressure or being behind an eight-ball. Hey, whatever. It's cool. This attitude alone will probably net this salesperson a few fresh deals by month's end. But, can you see how a salesperson's demeanor might be different if it's the 23rd of the month and they're sitting at two or three units? Yes, sir. A little stress, anxiety, worry, you name it. It sounds difficult, and it must be acknowledged and practiced, but if this underperforming salesperson could conjure up and utilize a little feigned indifference, you can bet the results by the end of the month would be better than if it hadn't been so. In just a bit, we'll talk about words that lend to feigned indifference.

Okay, second example: What about the customers of another salesperson? This one is dead on. Now depending on your individual pay plans and no matter what you might admit to yourself, you have a natural, be it small, amount of indifference when working with customers who are not yours. Why is this? Very little risk - high reward. It's human nature. If you don't close these people, you imagine the original salesperson can and will follow-up with them. You still get a "thank you" or a pat on the back for working with them. If you do close them, you might earn money (half the deal perhaps, again depending on pay plan), gain ½ unit, and you're a hero. It's good either way. I agree that this really isn't the way to look at the big picture, but you'd be amazed by how many actually do. The point is – harness this attitude and be able to use it at will.

The third way to acquire and utilize feigned indifference is through a little understanding and training. And that leads us to the second part of this section, The Technique.

THE TECHNIQUE

The many word tracks in this book are extremely effective on their own. If you do a great job and commit them all to memory and practice using them on a consistent basis, you will sell more vehicles. If you choose to make them part of your sales process along with the Technique described in this section, your words will be all the more powerful.

Let's breakdown the Technique... As stated earlier, we are always closing during the sales process. Again, whatever your process might be, there are steps to be followed. These steps are to be followed in order whenever possible. Some believe that the sales process used out of order guarantees the loss of a sale. While not a firm believer in this, I imagine that there must be a way to get back on track should your prospect wish to stray from the path. The Technique helps us do to this as well.

The Technique is as follows, and we should remember this well from the Introduction:

A prospect or customer voices an objection or concern. These can be direct or even appear in the form of a negative comment, which, of course, we will not take personally.

1. **Counter/Response**
2. **Analyze Prospect Reaction**
3. **Close or Third Party Example**
4. **Analyze Prospect Reaction**
5. **Close or Retreat/Pullback**
6. **Counter/Response**
7. **Repeat as necessary**

Now let us take a closer look at each of these shall we?

Step #1: Counter or Response to the concern or objection

When the prospect or customer brings up a concern you will pause briefly, nod, then counter immediately and confidently, all the while maintaining a pleasant demeanor. You are able to do this because you have practiced not taking anything personally. How will you counter? That depends entirely upon the concern. Every sales professional should be able to respond to any concern and do it the same way every time. We will go over all counters you need in future chapters, and it will be in depth. Use them all the time, every time.

Step # 2: Analyze Prospect Reaction

Once you have countered with a positive statement, you will quickly note the reaction of your prospect. This reaction will be one of these: Positive, Neutral, or Negative. Positive signs might include a nod, a smile, or a change in posture that exhibits a new interest. A neutral sign would be a blank stare or virtually no sign at all. A negative sign could be the shaking of the head, an inquisitive look that denotes a lack of understanding or believability, or simply appearing distracted. For those of you interested in advance study, there are numerous sources with varying ideas about how to read people. Any additional skills developed in this area will only add to your closing ability and income.

Step #3: Close or Use a Third Party Example

If the reaction to your counter is positive, you will close immediately. "Shall we continue then?" is wonderful if you are at an initial stage. This is especially valuable when moving to the presentation. If you are at the end of the sales process a "Shall we continue with the paperwork then" is a powerful and soft close. Or, "I will happily handle all of the details. Shall I consider you one of our valued customers?" And again, there are many closing statements available. The key is to choose one and use it always. Remember, consistency is powerful.

If the response of your prospect or customer was neutral or negative, you are going to roll right into a third-party example. A third-party example is one of the strongest re-inforcers available and they should always be used. Why are they so powerful? This is because you or a representative of your dealership is not the one relating the opinion.

So how could a third-party example work in this case? Let's assume a negative response: "That's more money than we wanted to spend." You respond with a nod and an "I understand." But then you continue, "In fact, just last week I had someone relate the very same feelings. But when they did some research, they discovered that the fuel efficiency alone would actually save them more than the difference in dollars from what they had originally budgeted."

Now this was just an example. A sales professional should create and study a *third-party example journal*. This will always keep these valuable tools at your disposal. And the neat thing is that they don't have to be your third-party examples. Stories that build value from other salespeople can be used effectively too. Moving on...

Step #4: Analyze Prospect Response

If you have utilized a third-party example at this time, take a look and study your prospect. Do you now see a positive response? A neutral one?

Step #5: Close or Repeat or Pullback

If you experience either one of these you will close right away: "Understanding this, shall we continue with the purchase? I'll take care of everything for you." Be positive and smile.

If you receive another negative reaction, "I said it's just too much money right now!" you will retreat or pull back immediately: "Of course, it's entirely up to you. You have to see the value in it."

Step #6: Counter/Response

Once you have pulled back and allowed the prospect to relax, you will counter again: "This being said..." The idea here is not to leave it alone quite yet. The beauty of the Technique, though, is that once it is mastered you will be able to close quickly and efficiently where you would not have before, and you will have happier customers and prospects.

Step #7: Repeat as necessary

Some have asked why the Technique is in the order it is written and why. For instance, why would one attempt to close from a positive response after the initial counter, but close on either a positive or neutral response to the third-party example? Good question.

The reason to use a third-party example after the first attempt to overcome the concern is because third-party examples are so effective that we should choose to utilize them as soon as possible.

The reason behind closing on a neutral response as well as a positive one after the third-party and prior to retreating or pulling back is simply that we *need* to ask for the business. There is no better way to get a true gauge on where the customer stands.

One of the most elegant explanations of the design of the The Technique was given by Brian Bursell, a sales consultant who was also an accomplished musician. He said that we practice the Technique as we would a musical scale. We practice the execution of the notes, and then we play the song. And as with different artists, the song takes on the individual nuances and styles of the performer. This is quite a profound and accurate description, far more profound and accurate than I could have created. Thank you Brian.

The Technique is simply a process for countering concerns and/or objections and closing on them quickly. And by closing, as repeated several times, I don't mean just the sale. We are always closing on the road to the sale. If someone does not want a professional presentation, we must eventually close them on that. If we present the vehicle, but they do not want to drive it, we have to close them on the idea of a demonstration. If they don't wish to go as far as a purchase consultation, well, you get the idea. The steps of The Technique were described at the very beginning of this program, and now we're going to get into it in detail. At the end of this chapter, you will find a chart that displays the flow of the Technique (this chart is from the original "You Don't Have To Say "No!" audio program developed in the mid-2000s for Saturn facilities). Please take a look at this from time to time as we continue. We are going to look at a couple of scenarios: the first will take place right after the welcome and a customer will have a concern about price before we are able to really do a presentation; the second will be during the write-up.

Example One: You have welcomed a customer to the store and have at least begun an interview outside (not the preferred place, but just the same, it's done). You are stopped at a pre-owned vehicle and the customer has a concern right off the bat. . .

"It says here that the price of this car is $9,973. That's too high. If I can buy it for nine grand out-the-door maybe I'll take it."

Now, you haven't had the chance to give your presentation and already he's trying you on for a pretty sizeable discount. It would be a simple matter here to show slight frustration, but remember not to take anything personally. Maintain your pleasant expression and counter immediately,

"John, when you say 'too high' do you mean too high for the vehicle or more than you wanted to spend?"

We have just pulled a counter you will learn in the next chapter. You will learn many more.

"It's too much for the vehicle," John says. "I can buy one down the street for a lot less."

We will use a tremendously powerful counter we will learn in the next chapter.

"Keep in mind John, all the reasons another dealership would sell a vehicle like this for less have already been addressed by us."

This is another opportunity for your individuality to shine through.

Now, watch his reaction. If it is positive – he says "I understand," or he nods in agreement or understanding, close right away. "Shall we continue and take a closer look at this car?"

If the response is neutral or negative, he seems indifferent or shakes his head or says something negative, use your experience to utilize a third party example.

"You know, John, I had a fella in last week that had a similar concern. But when he saw the value for the dollar, the fact that the condition of our vehicle was better and that the price was lower than others he had seen, he took delivery of his 2010 Impala that very day."

Analyze the reaction again. If it is positive or neutral, close. If it is negative, use feigned indifference and pull back or retreat.

Here are a few retreat or pull-back phrases:

1. **"It's your choice."**
2. **"You're in control."**
3. **"It's all up to you."**
4. **"You're the boss."**
5. **"Ultimately, it's your decision."**
6. **"We're here to serve you."**
7. **"I'm only here to help**

And what is it that pull-back or retreat phrases are designed to do? Well, they allow your customer to relax for a moment. Their defenses are able to drop. We're letting them gain control for a bit. Then, without the customer being fully aware of it, we take control again and close.

Here is an example of one of these in use:

"But, John, you have to see the value for yourself. The beautiful thing at our dealership is that you make the decisions, you're in control."

This time don't wait to analyze the reaction, counter quickly.

"That being said, dozens of educated consumers who have done their research buy pre-owned vehicles from us every month. Understanding this, let's take a closer look at this nice car."

Continue to repeat this process until John understands or is on the verge of discomfort. At discomfort, you really have only one option.

"Well, it's all up to you John. What would you like to do?"

What this question will do is hopefully have your customer believe they have regained control. You will then be able to restart the Technique.

Example Two: You have gotten to the write-up and are presenting numbers on a brand new car. You think you have everything under control. You believe to have built the necessary value, the bottom line is 28,987.42 but Jill is going to try you on. . .

"Okay. Looks great! You make it an even $27,000 and I'll take it right now."

If you sell with a One-Price philosophy, the vehicle has probably already been discounted and you will have to re-iterate the benefit of No-Hassle, No-haggle and stick to your guns. Now, if you are under a philosophy that will negotiate to a point, you will at least try to narrow the gap between your number and hers. We will not lose a deal over dollars if at all possible. But, our job as a salesperson is to hold as much gross profit as possible. And this does not happen by telling Jill that you have to go check with your manager right away.

Still smiling, counter right now...

"I appreciate that offer, Jill. However, as I mentioned earlier, we have found that this particular vehicle, with this equipment has been selling very well for very close to this figure."

Watch for her response. If positive, you close now. "Shall we continue with the paperwork then?" If neutral (no real response) or negative "It doesn't matter, that's what I'm paying!" go to a third party example. Maybe even pull back or retreat a little first.

"Of course. The beautiful thing is that it all up to you. This being said, many of my customers have found it easier to find a bit more in their budgets now, rather than to find out in a year or two, maybe less, that they

settled and have it cost them thousands to trade out of a vehicle they no longer want to drive."

Look at her. Analyze her reaction.

If positive or neutral – use a transitional statement and close. "Keeping this in mind, shall we finish the paperwork?" If negative, pull back and retreat. "As I said, you are in control Jill. You have to want the vehicle. If you see value in it, buy it. If not, take all the time you need."

If Jill looks like she's ready to go and you negotiate, don't leave it here. Immediately counter.

"Now Jill, as I said, we will not lose a deal over dollars. Your referrals and repeat business are very important to us. If you can come up to closer to the bottom line, I will happily take your offer to my manager."

Smile, and see what she says. Then attempt to move on.

Again, with a One-Price philosophy, go over this again with Jill. Also, for more, please refer to the <u>Famous Last Words</u> section of the Putting It All Together chapter.

Okay. . . these are just examples. Keep in mind, The Technique can be used all of the time: product knowledge, comparisons, concerns, etc. If we learn to use The Technique frequently, and in even newer ways (your individuality again), we will be able to close more and more of our customers. But, we have to believe. And use it even when it seems difficult. This is the key to our improvement.

Chapter In-Review

There was a very good reason to introduce Feigned Indifference and the Technique at this juncture of Beyond the Walkaround. That reason was to give you these materials prior to the majority of the word tracks being laid before you. As we progress and learn more, you will now be able to think of these word tracks differently. You will be able to understand them in a different light and consider a variety of usage circumstances and presentations.

1. **The True Purpose of Feigned Indifference.**

When we speak of Feigned Indifference, please remember that this is utilized not to seem dismissive of your customer, but to minimize the effectiveness of their potential defenses and/or negativity. You must still portray the undeniable desire to help them buy a vehicle.

2. **Use The Technique When Necessary, But With Discretion.**

The Technique is not meant to be used to talk the customer to death or to give them no room to move, rather it is utilized to close from concerns or objections when possible. *Remember the idea given by the musician and practice your scales every day.*

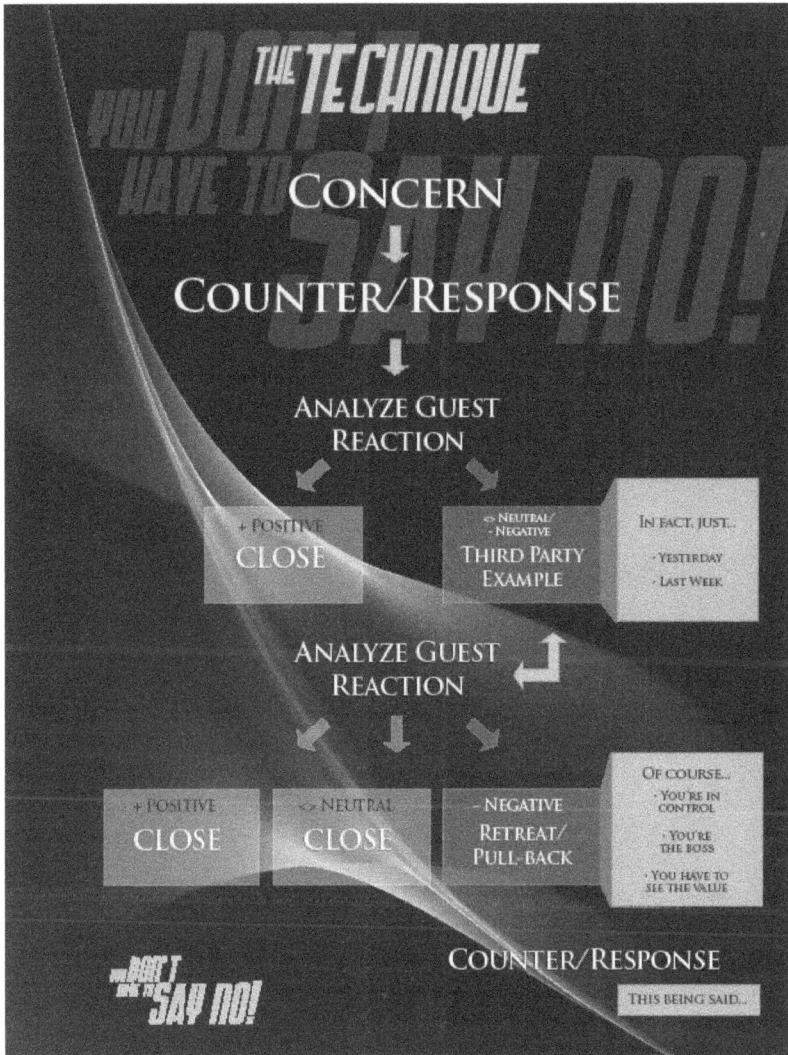

THE TECHNIQUE

CONCERN

↓

COUNTER/RESPONSE

↓

ANALYZE GUEST REACTION

+ POSITIVE	⟷ NEUTRAL/ − NEGATIVE	IN FACT, JUST...
CLOSE	THIRD PARTY EXAMPLE	· YESTERDAY · LAST WEEK

ANALYZE GUEST REACTION

+ POSITIVE	⟷ NEUTRAL	− NEGATIVE	OF COURSE...
CLOSE	CLOSE	RETREAT/ PULL-BACK	· YOU'RE IN CONTROL · YOU'RE THE BOSS · YOU HAVE TO SEE THE VALUE

COUNTER/RESPONSE

THIS BEING SAID...

BEYOND THE WALKAROUND

Addressing Price Concerns (New and Used)

We are now going to venture into the world of overcoming price particulars. There will be specific word tracks introduced in this chapter that, alone, if practiced and used consistently will close you deals. After these, and the subsequent word tracks introduced in the Trade-Ins and Payments chapters, have been gone over, you will really get an idea of how powerful the concept of Feigned Indifference can be. This comes together very clearly. As we put all of these things together and your own style begins to emerge, you will see how Feigned Indifference and the Technique can be utilized to their greatest extent.

Even though some of you might work under a strict selling system such as a four-square or a modified four-square, we are going to address price concerns separately, trade-in concerns separately, and payment and down payment concerns separately. This is so that the remainder of us who are not under any specific selling system will be able to benefit and use these concepts whenever they might come up. Now, obviously, a four-square is presented, in most settings, by showing the retail figure with some accessory or package of accessories added so that you are beginning at a figure that is in some cases several hundreds of dollars over list price. You show the trade-in value, then quote a high short-term payment, coupled with, of course, a large down payment. This is designed for one thing: generate an offer. If you have done your job on the presentation, demonstration and everything else along the road to the sale, and the customer is ready to buy, you will find a way, in most cases, to make it work for your customer. The key is to hold as much gross profit as possible. This is done by utilizing the tactics and word tracks that we will discuss in the following sections. You will discover that everything we will learn increases the value of the deal as a package and reduces your need to give up your money. We will go over an example presentation or two later in the program. Now, let's analyze the price issues:

The primary thing we need to remember when it comes to price is that when a customer questions you or shows concern over the dollar amount you are asking for the vehicle, or vehicles in general, you musn't take it personally. You do recall when I mentioned this before? Well, here it is again. I understand that it's difficult to do at times. I mean why wouldn't you take it personally? You have used one or all of the five positive-value statements to explain why our vehicle is worth the money and to help set up the negotiation; you are a professional in the business and if anyone knows the price your vehicle should sell for, it's you; and further, how could anyone who buys a vehicle every three or four years possibly know anything? Right? Right. Wrong. This is out-of-date. There is far too much accessible information out there for our customers. Maybe time for another mind-set change… This information can actually be of benefit to us and we need to look at it this way. We can't come to the conclusion that the customers and the internet sites are out to get us. It'll take us off our game. Some of you might have never had these types of thoughts pop into your head. Some of you might feel pangs of indignation more than you'll admit. If you do, you should heed the soon to be immortal sales person decree **"Don't take it personally!"** Further, I imagine many of you have heard the common, though outdated, philosophy that we, as sales professionals have the clear advantage over the customer because we do this for a living. Get this out of your head. You don't need to believe this to have the confidence you need to be the best. The truth of the matter is this: you need to be highly-skilled and trained to even be on a level playing field with a good percentage of your customers. The sheer number of choices available to them, the fantastic amount of information at their disposal through the internet we mentioned before (don't forget misinformation – there is plenty of that), and the simple fact that they really don't *need* to buy a vehicle from you gives them an initial advantage. It is solely up to us to make them love our products and feel comfortable doing business with us. In short, make them *want* to buy the vehicle from you. Anyway let's move on . . .

Now, what we will do next is examine some of the more common concerns that our customers might bring up. The object here is to be able to respond confidently, quickly, and calmly. And, don't forget to avoid any **visible signs of frustration** on your part. These signs might include one or all of the following: **clenched jaw, pursed lips, a furrowed brow, narrowing eyes, drooping shoulders...** you get the idea. Also remember, once you respond to a concern, it is your goal that your customer will have one of two reactions. Remember, they will hopefully either *understand* the meaning behind the statement or they will ask "What do you mean?" "What do you mean" will allow you to fortify your reasoning and follow with one or more of the set-ups or transitional phrases and closing questions or statements we discussed in the Preparing For Purchase Consultation chapter, or third-party examples of your own. This was again discussed a bit last in the chapter describing the Technique.

What about another method long thought to teach us to isolate the concern or objection? You might know which one I'm talking about – the method that includes the phrase "other than." An example being: "Other than price, is there any reason you would not purchase the vehicle." I believe in this, but obviously a consultant must choose the situation properly and not abuse the phrase. It is most effective if used almost as an afterthought near the customer's perceived end of the visit, where they might give you information that could provide the means to close the sale. Perhaps they will give you a real, solid objection. Another good spot might be following a trial close. You could be able to solidify your position. But, you know what I'm getting at with the abuse part. "Other than the price, is there any reason you would not purchase the vehicle." The customer responds: "Yes. The color is not one I would have chosen." "Okay, other than the price and the color, is there any reason you wouldn't buy this now?" "Yeah, I wanted a sunroof too." "All right, so other than the price, the color, and the fact that it doesn't have a sunroof, is there any other reason you wouldn't take this car?" "I really could use an automatic." "Sigh. Okay, start over. Other than . . . "   Yes, I know that this salesperson must have done a rotten job during the interview, if one was even done, and I know that it's a bit comical, but it's also the way some people are trained. I know because I had such a stimulating role-play session with a sales manager some years ago. It became painfully clear, as it now has for you, that the "other than" technique was his favorite. Now, **other than**, the fact that this method can be seen as a bit transparent and mechanical, please keep in mind, too, that the salesperson must be careful that his or her "other than" does not minimize the concern or you might generate an irritated customer that comes back with:

"Isn't the fact that the price is too high enough?"

If this does occur, you had better empathize and tell them just how legitimate that concern is. Of course, there are ways to deal with this particular price obstacle, which we will go over here shortly. Let's, for now, begin with some basics and then work our way through some more. I know, there is a lot of material presented here, but the material must be mastered before any advanced methods, such as the Technique, can be effective.

What I'd like to do is begin with some common concerns. These will come up consistently when working with your customers. Of course, there will be plenty more. It is for this reason that it is highly recommended, again, that every salesperson keep a *concerns journal along with a third-party example section*. We will continue to talk about when and how third-party examples are best used. But for now, let us begin. . .

You might have just completed your interview and taken the customer to the lot, or, you might be starting a write up, and you hear: "The price is too high" or "This is too much money."

This is a fair statement on the part of the customer and it could refer to either a new or a pre-owned vehicle. And similar to "Just looking", it could also be a conditioned response born of fear. Or it could be a strategy used in the attempt to set up a discount and/or a negotiation. And remember, every time you are able to counter effectively you are building value and comfort and lowering expectation with regard to a discount. This leads to more sales and higher profits.

Your response must be immediate and confident.

"When you say the price is too high, do you mean it is too high for the vehicle or it's more than you would like to spend?"

You are isolating without going directly to "other than." And, don't worry about planting a bad seed by asking if they think the price is too high for the vehicle. We can easily overcome this, and better to get it out now. You are also able to discover if the objection is value-based or related to budget. This will give us a better idea about how to counter.

Your customer will, more than likely, answer one way or the other.

If they respond "This is too much for the vehicle," we, of course, have a value issue and you should say something similar to the following:

For new, you can re-state a pre-emptive strike or one of our basic positive value statements:

"Well the good news is that these vehicles have been selling very, very well for this figure, maybe a little more."

You then transition: **"Knowing this…"**

Close, either to a presentation: **"Let's take a closer look at this vehicle."**

Or to the paperwork, if at the desk: **"Would you prefer to take delivery at 4 or 5 this evening?"**

Now, it is understood that the pricing of new vehicles has, in fact increased rather than decreased. The value, however, as always, is superior. If the next step or deal is not closed, you can follow with this:

"It is interesting, too, that in comparisons to similar vehicles on the market and because of our great factory pricing, our products generally come in lower than the other makes."

Again, you then transition: **"Considering this…"**

Close, either to a presentation: **"Let me show you why this vehicle is so special."**

Or to the paperwork, if at the desk: **"Let's continue with the paperwork."**

Hopefully, you will get a "what do you mean?" or a "Really?" on the lot, but even if you get an "I don't believe that!" You're okay. And, of course, if at the desk, you want an "I understand" or a realistic offer.

And if the customer does give you that "I don't believe it!" you just respond with enthusiasm, **"Well, it's true. Let me show you why!"**

Another way to handle the price is too high for the new vehicle is to counter with this...

"Well, the prices haven't gone up as much as people might think. You'd be surprised to know that the new _____, for instance, with all of its features is priced less than a _____was in 2013! Here let me show you. . . Dollar for dollar, value for value, you still get more vehicle than you did years ago!

Now, what you are doing here is showing that, in some cases, the pricing really hasn't climbed too much.

One thing I would recommend is that you be on the lookout for trade-ins that still have the original Monroney sticker. Save them, copy them for your teammates and make comparisons. They can be invaluable. You really wouldn't believe the MSRPs on some of these vehicles. You should still be able to make a strong point. These old window stickers are great for an evidence manual or a brag book. For those of you unfamiliar with an evidence manual or a brag book, it is simply a scrapbook of sorts. It is put together for your customer. It gives them something to look at while otherwise idle. The book should have examples of other happy customers, testimonials, specials, etc. Your managers and some of your veterans will be able to help you with this. Please learn to use all of your resources.

If none of these are able to transition you to a close or at least the opportunity to build more value, we can counter with the following in order to pull some more information from the customer:

"These vehicles (at this price) have done very well for us. What have you read or heard that is keeping you from seeing the value when so many others have?"

Many of these are interchangeable with respect to new or used.

Let's go back to the "This is too much money" objection. What if the customer says that it's more than he wanted to spend? We can counter effectively like this...

"John, when you say it's more than you wanted to spend, do you plan to pay cash or finance?"

If it's cash, use the following:

"John, it's your hard-earned money. You ultimately have to see value in the vehicle. Also, please understand that there is no relationship between what you might have budgeted and what this vehicle is worth or what it will ultimately sell for."

This should certainly achieve our "I understand" or "What do you mean?"

If the response is "I understand", you should attempt to move on to close the next step whether it be the presentation/demonstration or the write-up.

If the response is "What do you mean?" you can use an effective third-party example that will be revisited during the section on Payments and that has already been touched upon with the Technique...

"Just the other day, one of my very good customers found that it was easier to find a little more in her budget now, rather than discover in a year or two that she settled for a vehicle she didn't really want only to have it cost her thousands to trade out of it."

As has been stated, this counter will be used later in the payment and down payment section. It is highly effective for either total dollar concerns or payments. Frequently, people are unaware of how the total amount financed is related to payments at various terms and rates.

Then close:

"Knowing this, shall we continue with the paperwork?"

If your goal is met, that being the customer either agreeing to sign the paperwork or proposing a reasonable offer – keep in mind that it's your responsibility to continue using the countering word tracks until something of this sort is met – then you have done your job. If not, keep going.

In case you haven't gathered, you have been using a portion of the Technique in this chapter. And we will continue to do so throughout the book.

If the reply is that they wish to finance, the customers are assuming a payment based on what an outside source has told them they could finance or what payment a bottom line would give them. These things often fall under the column of misinformation and will require a little digging on your part to figure things out. A good follow to this, however, is:

"Great! Who do you bank through and what did they tell you a vehicle like this or this total dollar amount would run you every month?"

This will help you learn a little about your customer. Again, some folks don't know or understand how bottom line, term, or rate can relate to a monthly payment. Further investigation might reveal that you are right where they would like to be; because, frankly, they will probably be able to answer the first question but not the second. Some facilities prefer that you avoid getting an idea about what figure your customer has targeted, either out-the-door, trade-in or payment because it is believed that this locks you in to some degree. Others want you to get a little more info.

Another dealership representing your manufacturer might be advertising a discount on a model or models that yours is not. It might not be exactly the same unit from an equipment standpoint, or it might be a unit produced prior to a price increase, or they're just emptying their guns on a loss leader. We should still attempt to counter this before going to management. It will save us gross in the future.

"All _____s are priced the same from the manufacturer with the very same mark-up, so I am unable to say exactly what the difference might be other than color, equipment, or miles – if it was a demonstrator, I do have those for you. For us, these vehicles are selling very well at the figure I will present to

you. In the meantime, I would be happy to have my manager research the vehicle you saw. Do you remember where you saw it? What color was it? And what was the price?"

Try to do this without seeming like you are interrogating your customer. I know - it can sure seem like it! Remember, we don't want to do this with pre-owned either. But, in a case such as this, the information is necessary.

Tell your manager the situation and work together to close the deal. This situation will not arise often, but it is always wise to be prepared.

Now, on to the pre-owned vehicle . . .

We are going to cover many possibilities here, the reason being that there is certainly a big opportunity to improve the used car business and profitability of virtually all retail facilities in the country. Your personal income will grow dramatically if you are able to counter the majority of used car concerns.

Now, if your customer comes right out and exclaims "this is too much for this vehicle!" Remember, that this could be a defense, or perhaps they are attempting to set up a negotiation. Maybe, though, they have actually seen a similar vehicle priced for less, maybe on the internet, or perhaps they have been shot a low number at another dealership. If you respond the way you do for new vehicles, your customer very well might tell you why he feels this way. If he doesn't and reiterates his concern about the price being too high, you are going to respond quietly, calmly "That's a fair statement, John. Why do you feel that this is so?"

John should reply in one way or another. He will either give you a reason or he will say "I don't know – I just think so" or something similar. He might say that he saw one down the street or on the internet just like it priced for less. We'll attack that in a bit. But, for now, let's stick to "I don't know" or "I just think so."

Your response is simple if he says he really doesn't know. You will explain how the vehicles are priced and hope to build a level of confidence:

"Well, you will be pleased to know that the majority of our vehicles are priced either at or below what similar vehicles with similar miles and equipment sell for in this market. This provides everyone the same opportunity and value. We believe that everyone is important and we treat them that way. Let me to show you why this vehicle is worth the money."

A version of this response can obviously be used if someone asks us how we arrive at our prices, or how we price our vehicles - market-based pricing.

If the customer says "no," to your request to let you show them the vehicle, you respond.

"Then let's look at some more vehicles. We'll find one you like. Don't worry."

And attempt to move on. This might take the vehicle away in a particular manner. They might say "Well, let's take a look at this one. That makes sense." Again, always have something positive to say.

If our customer presses you and asks, "Well, what can you do for me on this one?" again, instead of offering a discount or going straight to your manager, use one of the five positive value statement from last section...

"I will be happy to provide you with a wonderful bottom line for this unit, if it is, in fact, one you would like to own. Keeping this in mind, shall we take a closer look at the vehicle?"

Then attempt to show the vehicle again. If you are able to accomplish this, you have just increased your likelihood of delivering this unit, and you have certainly increased your gross profit.

What if our friend John is one of those discount buyers, the kind who needs a discount no matter how the vehicle is priced, and says the following?

"Dealer XYZ will give me $500-$1,000 off for just walking in the door. Will you offer this too?"

Now, what I'm going to do is give you four responses. Keep in mind that by having an immediate response that does not deny the customer's claims, you will support your position without saying "No they didn't," which calls your customer out as a liar. There is no good way to catch your customer in a lie. They lose face, and this, of course, makes them uncomfortable. If the customer leaves after losing face, the chance of a return is almost zero. Also, you will not have to interrogate them or make them prove their claim, which is confrontational, again making them uncomfortable. After stating these, we're going to go over each one of them in detail. So here they are:

1. **"If a vehicle is priced correctly, no adjustment should be necessary."**
2. **"Either they, themselves, believe the price is too high or the vehicle is not quite right somehow."**
3. **"Unfortunately, it seems that they are struggling with the value of their vehicle for some reason."**
4. **"Please don't allow a misconception to prevent you from saving money."**

The first statement, **"If a vehicle is priced correctly, no adjustment should be necessary,"** is not meant to be sarcastic, but, again, it's all how we communicate the idea. There are ways to say these things. Other salespeople are not concerned with how things are said, but we will be. There is a difference. "If the car is priced right, we shouldn't have to discount it!" It's all how it's said. There is always a message. The message is either: "You don't know what you're talking about" or "I understand, but the vehicle is simply worth it." Which one would you rather convey? Oh, by the way, saying **"I understand, but the vehicle is simply worth it"** is a strong, strong statement. Particularly if it is followed by a quick retreat: "But keep in mind, it's all up to you. You have to see the value." Then right to a close, "If you do see the value as most do, why don't we continue with the paperwork?" Nice, eh? You've again just heard a bit of The Technique. It works. This counter, or a form of this counter, is also effective for someone asking for either a specific (I need you to take

$1,200 off or I need to be at $11,000 out-the-door) or a non-specific (What will you take off the price?) like so...

"We try to price our vehicles so that very little adjustment is ever necessary. This vehicle is worth every dollar and more."

Now, number two, **"Either they themselves believe the price is too high, or the vehicle is not quite right somehow,"** states that the other dealership has no confidence in their product. Perhaps they do not feel that the unit will, again, bring the money that they are asking. We must be confident. Our vehicles are worth the money, they have value. They are reconditioned. They are ready to go. We do not wish to have our customers spend their hard-earned money only to have them shell out hundreds more in maintenance like others expect them to do.

Number Three, **"Unfortunately, it seems that they are struggling with the value of their vehicle for some reason,"** is just another way to say the same thing. The power is having a number of similar statements to support our philosophy, to make our customers understand.

The fourth statement here, **"Don't allow a misconception to cost you money"** or you can say **"to prevent you from saving money,"** is meant to bring a shadow of doubt into everything another sales consultant might say or do. And what kind of misconception might our customers run into? There can be a bunch. For instance, they are receiving a discount on a vehicle that is two thousand dollars overpriced to begin with, or is distressed in some way through age or lack of reconditioning. No matter which direction you take, a great follow-up is this:

"Whatever it might be, I'm glad you are here. You'll be treated well and always get more than what you pay for."

We are also able to combine the five positive value statements with some of these words track to create effective closes. You have done a remarkable job staying off price, building value, and limiting the customer's exaggerated discount ideas. And while you have used your word tracks, this person will not cave, perhaps saying something like the following:

"C'mon, you're not giving me anything. Give me something and we have a deal."

You respond solidly...

"I can appreciate that you feel you're not getting anything, John. But, in fact, because of the way we do business, and knowing now that this particular vehicle, with this equipment has been selling very well for very close to this figure, what did you have in mind? Another tank of gas, an oil change?"

The next concern can also occur during the presentation of the numbers, but it might occur beforehand.

"That's more than I wanted to spend. If you take $_____ off, we'll take it."

While this is an offer and a somewhat positive situation, they are obviously either not 100% sold or they are just trying us on. You have to reinforce the value of the vehicle. If they press or seem dissatisfied, say this (you will recognize it from a similar version just a short while ago):

"Please understand that we respect you and your desire to spend your hard-earned money with us. I will tell you, though, that many of our customers have found it less difficult to find a little more money in their budget now rather than discover in a year or two, or less, that they settled and then have it cost them thousands to trade out of the unit. If you can – please buy the vehicle you want to this time."

This can be extremely effective and will help with new vehicles as well.

Okay, these will get you back on the road to the sale more often than not.

All of these will work with any selling philosophy. The difference, clearly, with one-price is that you will already have a discounted or market-priced unit and you simply will not come off that price. The word tracks learned in this book will help you close the deals on these vehicles without discounting, or you will minimize the discount in the case of negotiation.

Understand that there *will* be situations where you simply cannot explain away a price difference. There might be a current year or late model that is an aged unit at another store - though there is probably a reason why it is aged. Maybe there is a reconditioning or cosmetic issue. In off-brand situations, perhaps the other dealership sells that vehicle new and was able to take it in on trade well or purchase it at a factory sale to which we have no access. I don't know. There might be a number of causes. These are rare instances. Talk to your manager and discuss tactics, understanding that these things will happen from time to time.

A concern that is one we'll hear more often than we should, because, quite frankly, it's rather silly, is the following: "I'll just go to the big city (whatever it might be)." The understanding is, of course, that the larger dealerships are able to sell for less because of the volume they do. Your response is simply this:

"If it were truly a better deal to go to the city, I would think the word would have gotten out.   And, if so, how is it that we do such a great business here. In fact, if it were true, how would anyone in this town sell any cars at all?"

And just as ridiculous is the opposite philosophy: "I'll just go to the smaller town and buy. They have lower overhead and don't have the expenses." Your response is a quick one:

"Haven't you considered that because of their lower volume, these dealership must strive for higher profits just to pay the bills? And, if it were the case that they sell for less, don't you think that word would have gotten out? Why would we do the great business we do?"

And certainly these small dealerships would not remain small, would they?

Anyway, what happens if someone has been looking at what they perceive to be an identical used car? They might say something like:

"I can buy the same car down the street for $1000 less."

You respond with confidence:

"All the reasons another dealership would sell a vehicle like this for less have already been addressed by us."

We introduced this briefly a bit earlier in the book. This is a very strong statement. After all, it implies that there is some mechanical or cosmetic issue that has not been corrected. It implies that the other dealership would rather save money on reconditioning in the hope that the customer will not suffer consequences for some time to come. And it justifies our price if we have used the statement mentioned last section. You might follow a "What do you mean?" by a:

"Well, whether it be mechanical or cosmetic, I couldn't say. But clearly, it's one of these things."

A good follow:

"After all, I would not want to see you have to put hundreds of dollars in basic maintenance into your vehicle within the first 30 days or so. That would take a lot away from the experience, and we want you completely satisfied."

A little more:

"Please understand that I do not make my living selling a single car. I need you to be able to recommend

your friends, your family, and I need you to want to buy from me again. Your whole experience is important."

What about a customer who is shopping you against a private owner? Well, most of those owners are trying to sell for retail, as we are, because they believe they weren't offered enough on trade. But, effective counters, and a form of these will be used next section when trade-ins are focused upon, are as follows:

"First and foremost, if it were truly the best way to purchase a pre-owned unit, there would be little need for retail used car sales. Also, the classified sections of the newspapers would have long ago been as thick as telephone books, but they aren't, are they?"

Another:

"And, of course, John you would carry all of the responsibility. The private owner can't provide you with an inspected or certified vehicle; they can't provide warranty options or financing options, and the only person to go to if anything goes wrong is back to the seller – and their resources and desires are limited. That is why people buy from us."

Here is a really tough one and a rare one, but let's go over the scenario.

"According to what I have read (looked at), all of your prices are way too high."

"I understand, John. When you say 'all of our vehicles,' do you mean 'all' or just the one you are comparing? And when you say 'looked at,' do you mean other dealerships, market reports, or the internet?"

"The internet. Mostly Kelley Blue Book and Edmund's. They both said the car should sell for less."

"That doesn't surprise me, would you like to know why?"

If "No," you ask "Why would you say this?" or "Why not?"

If "Yes. . ."

"Kelley and Edmund's are sources, much like Black Book or NADA. If all the sources were accurate, they wouldn't differ as much as they do, and they do, don't they?"

"Yeah, they do. But still, they *all* say you're priced too high."

"This really is a unique situation. But understand that there is a certain dollar amount that is required to trade for a vehicle like this or to be the highest bidder at auction. If we believe that this will fill a need for one of our customers, we need to pay that price no matter what the internet says."

"That doesn't help me in this case."

"John, you have to see the value. Please keep in mind that we deliver dozens of fine pre-owned vehicles here every month to educated consumers who have done their research. How could this be if our prices, clearly marked for all to see, were too high?"

If your prices are not clearly marked, simply remove that part of the word track.

Okay, if you get into a bind and really have a tough one, they might say something like this:

"If you won't take less or discount your vehicle, there is no point in going further!"

This is tough, but slow them down if you can. Make them explain their actions and reactions, and attitude for that matter.

"Why would you say this?"

Say this almost incredulously and with a smile as though you have never heard it before. The customer might just be surprised enough to continue speaking with you.

Hopefully they will respond with something we have already covered or that you have noted from a prior experience and written in your concerns journal.

Lastly on this subject, for now anyway, I would like to give you a wonderful counter to a concern that some have about paying full sticker, or what their perception of full sticker might be. . . This comes from one very talented sales consultant I have had the pleasure of working with named Dan Marsh. This one is also valuable for the "you're asking too much" or "the price is too high" concern.

"I never pay full sticker!"

"Well, John, we post all of our inventory on our website. We have had people drive 100 miles and more to take advantage of a good price. I know that they had to drive by other cars of the same description to get here. People like yourself wouldn't do that if we asked too much for our cars."

Use a transitional phrase, then ask to continue.

Before we move forward, one obstacle we failed to address was "I have to think about it." This can crop up almost from the word go. You can have someone say this right after you explain our philosophy to them. For now, I will tell you that no matter where they say this along the road to the sale, the goal, obviously, is to find out to what they must devote all of this thought. If you say something to the effect of "What do you have to think about?" it might sound a bit confrontational. At this point and while you are mastering your word tracks from this program, simply use this:

"I understand. Good percentages of my people are analytical and feel they have to think about a thing or two. What will you give the most thought to when you leave here, John, price, trade-in, payment, or down-payment?"

This does two things: "When you leave here" has the same effect as does "Before you go. . ." Both of these represent Feigned Indifference and a bit of a retreat. And, if and when, the customer gives you an answer, you might be able to use some of the word tracks and The Technique to overcome the concern and close the sale. Either way, you are in a better place.

Now we are going to cover some interesting and tight situations we might get into involving pricing done through conventional advertising (television, radio, newspaper) as well as through the internet – your website, e-mail, etc. You can bet that if your dealership advertises loss leaders, vehicles that are either aged, equipped sparsely or demonstrators, your competition is doing the same thing. There are a few, not many, facilities that will not quote a price over the internet; some have gone so far with the phone long ago. We will analyze how to engage the customer on the internet in a later chapter. As has been stated and made perfectly clear, please follow the philosophy given to you by your management team. And also remember that this book is not a comprehensive and complete road to the sale endeavor. We will find it satisfactory to address customer concerns that arise in the facility, face-to-face, in this chapter. These very same ideas can still build value and save gross over the phone and the internet.

One tactic that was developed in 1999, just about the time the internet was really rearing Its head, was that of complimenting or thanking your customer for doing their research. I was a floor manager at a Hyundai dealership when I began seeing an influx in print-outs of equipment, invoices, buying practices, what-have-you. How would I avoid completely giving the car away? First off, I would begin, when confronted with folks who claimed they knew what I paid for my vehicle, with this:

"Mr. and Mrs. Jones, thank you so much for taking the time to do your research. I have found with little exception that the more educated the consumer, the more likely they will buy from us today!"

This is quite an effective compliment and plays to their intellect and ability to secure a great buy. The second very powerful word track is the following:

"If you have done such a thorough job researching your vehicle, you have probably come across some of the buying sites that make clear that an offer of 3% to 4% above invoice is an extremely fair one that will probably and should be accepted if obtained, am I right?"

You can adjust this at your store. Even if you price at $300-$400 over invoice rather than a percentage, it will work well. This will help you actually make some gross on those who would be asking to drop below invoice or of course that magic $100 over invoice figure. You must always be smiling and enthusiastic and firm when reciting these ideas. Practice, as with anything, is a must.

This brings us to our next specific: What about those customers asking for even more off of an advertised special that your store is running? This can be either a new or used vehicle. Whether or not there is ultimately more room, you must be able to hold fast.

"I appreciate your asking, really. Please know, however, that this vehicle was advertised or quoted at this price for a reason… You're here because this represents a fantastic value. Understanding this, why don't we continue with the paperwork?"

You are able to use other word tracks or ideas in conjunction with this one. These would include the five statements in the Preparing For Purchase Consultation chapter. I recall an instance where several of these were used, in the form of the Technique, and we were prepared to let him go. Finally, the customer said, "Anything? Can you give me anything – a pizza coupon? Anything?" We had won. We gave him two free oil changes to bring him back to our service department and he took the car. Simple, Easy, Done.

Another powerful idea is that people want to feel they've won. "I want to win!" they either say it, think it, or feel it. Hyundai used this to their advantage with the "You Win" campaign in the early 2000's.

"You have won!" you tell these people, "You are the very first to this car at this price. Take it while you can. Let's do the paperwork (continue with the process)."

Further, you can suggest this fully to the buyer...

"Everyone wants to feel they've gotten something extra, something more. They want to win. You have won! You've won this vehicle at this price, because you were the first to see it, the first to want it. You've won. Buy the car."

"Why would we advertise a high price? It would be foolish! You've won. Buy the car!"

"Don't look for a discount for discounts sake."

One of the best ways to overcome a discount for discount sake is the APPLE STORY... In my right hand I have a crisp, good-looking apple that I have priced for 5 cents; in my left hand is a very similar apple, just as good-looking that I have priced for 3 cents. Now, because I like you, I'll go ahead and sell you the apple in my right hand for four cents. Are you going to buy that apple because I have discounted it 20 whole percent? Of course not, that would be foolish. You're going to buy the 3 cent apple because you're getting more for less. Seeing this clearly, shall we…." You understand.

Now let's talk about rebates… Or even, lease specials. If a customer is talking about how a competitor is offering better rebates or lease payments, we do have a counter… We have to help the customer understand that the reason these dollars or lease payments are available on this vehicle is because *that is what the manufacturer believes it will take to move the unit.* If this is the case, what is the vehicle really worth? The higher the rebate or more attractive the lease - the less valuable the unit. The idea is that even the manufacturer believes that the model is not worth the dollar that they are asking. We will, of course, abstain from this argument if our manufacturer is offering the better incentives.   Depending upon the rapport you have with your customer, a bold counter is this:

"How much less do you want your vehicle to be worth when you get it home? Pay now, or pay later. Ours will carry a better resale. If it is what you want, then buy it."

Chapter In-Review

In summation, everything in this section, all of the ideas and word tracks, are designed to give you something to say immediately that will slow your customer down and build value at the same time. Your responses must be swift and confident. But they must also be followed with the attempt to close the stage you are currently hoping to conclude. Also, it is fully understood that at some point, hopefully during the write-up, you will have to entertain an offer. All of the words and ideas presented up to this point are designed to increase that offer. If a few words can net you even a hundred dollars here or two hundred there... then they, the words, and you, have done the job.

1. This Is Part of the Beginning of Becoming the Best

We really began to look at a lot of situational material. We have studied how to overcome and counter objections and concerns for both new and used. Our real growth will come when we work with these every day. The time will come when the anxiety leaves you. And that will be a great day!

2. "All the reasons another dealership would sell a vehicle like this for less have already been addressed by us."

I wanted to re-emphasize this particular counter. This one was created years and years ago while I, another sales manager, and my General Manager were coming back from an all-company meeting. The point is this: we were still discussing the car business and thinking and role-playing. The best meetings are those that keep you going for a while after they're finished. Do these things with your teammates and see what comes of it. This word track has always been one of my favorites and most effective.

BEYOND THE WALKAROUND

Trade-Ins

There are many salespeople who will contend that overcoming the trade-in value is the most difficult part of the entire deal. It is in response to this belief that this comprehensive chapter was written. So sit back, and enjoy. This will be informative and fun. Let's start from scratch on trade-ins:

While we would love to have everything work in perfect harmony, this is seldom the situation. Here would be an example of this: you and your customer arrive back at your facility after the demonstration drive, you receive an enthusiastic positive response to your trial close, and you then say something like "Wonderful. It is now time for the trade evaluation process where we will place a value on your vehicle. Is that all right with you?" And your customer responds "I can't wait. I know you'll give me everything I want and I will, of course, buy my new car right now!" As great as this would be, particularly if it were to occur on a consistent basis, this doesn't normally happen quite this way.

What do we do with the customer who seems to jump out of his car saying "What'll ya give me for this?" Or the one who says "I want to drive this car," tosses you the keys to his and says "Have your manager drive this while I'm gone." We need to slow these folks down a bit. In the first case, we can try to do this with a word track we will use later in a somewhat similar situation. Your customer asks you "What'll ya give me for this?" and you respond:

"Every dollar it's worth and probably a little more!"

Then introduce yourself and welcome the customer to your store. Do your qualification and attempt to begin an interview with the common, maybe dated, but useful:

"Well John, what do you like about your trade-in that you have to have in your next vehicle or are you looking for something entirely different?"

And here's a quick tactic to put into your repertoire: If any customer makes a statement that they don't know what their looking for, you respond right away:

"If you don't know what you're looking for, I have the perfect vehicle for you!"

Then, begin showing them the *car of the day*, something you or your manager have selected, or something new and exciting. The key is to have a vehicle in mind. If they allow you to show the unit, they will either be enthused or they will, many times, open up and tell you what they are really looking for.

The second situation may be handled differently depending on the step on the road to the sale in which you're currently involved. If it happens right off the bat, then a response would be:

"Of course, while we're getting the keys to this vehicle, you can tell me a bit about your trade."

Then you simply begin to walk inside. If it occurs after you have presented a vehicle, the stars are aligning for you.

No matter if it is the perfect time to talk about the trade or if it is not and you cannot avoid it, here is a great transition word track:

"That's the easiest (or simplest) part of the entire process. What I'd like to do now is gather as much information about your vehicle as I can. What we will then do is utilize all the sources and market data available to us. That way, you will be provided with the highest available dollar for your trade-in. Is that all right (OK) with you?"

Then you proceed to *completely* fill out a trade appraisal form, including, of course, name, address, and phone number. If your customer is the one who is less than cooperative and asks why you need all this information, you reply:

"I have found that the more information I have, the better the appraisal, generally."

Then try to continue… If the customer pushes the issue and asks why you need an address and/or phone #, he/she might be one of the 5% who don't even want to give their name, you respond:

"If you're concerned about your information, I have a privacy notice here for you to sign."

In fact, for the sake of compliance, many dealer groups have privacy notices signed every time, and first thing in many cases, as part of a solid sales process.

<u>SILENT WALKAROUND</u>

The silent walkaround is an oldie, but a goodie! By the way, there is an Active Walkaround for customer trade-ins. The "active" part is getting the customer involved. Surprisingly, this is the part of the silent walkaround that is not silent. Without being too confusing, they're both pretty much the same thing. Interestingly, I have worked in a store that didn't want the salesperson anywhere near the trade-in. The idea being that the customer could not then hold that consultant responsible for the number they were getting. Let's face it though, if the situation is set up properly, most customers will understand that it is not the consultant placing the number. *In fact, we will learn to portray the many sources and current market place as the responsible party – not anyone at the store.*

Back to the silent walkaround . . . Do what your management team has deemed to be the best method. Again, there are stores that won't do it and there are some that require the activity before they even talk about the vehicle.

For those who do this or for those who would like to start, let's describe the task, shall we?

Once you have received permission to look at the trade, or have been asked to do so, grab your clipboard with your appraisal sheet and simply say, "Let's go look at your vehicle!" Be enthused (but not overly so). Be enthused no matter if the trade-in is a late model, a high-miler, an old clunker, etc. We certainly don't need to be jumping to any conclusions about how much the customer owes or what we think they'll need out of it. In fact, if you can pull off a vision of sugar plum fairies or something similar, you'll thank yourself later.

You and your customer go out to the trade-in and then you simply begin walking around it. Get the customer involved . . . **"John, would you read me the exact mileage off the odometer please?"** A common tactic is that you ask this while you write the vehicle identification number directly from the vehicle. This effective activity or step is, again, not new, but it is so often skipped or ignored.

Moving around, you will stop and note dents, dings, scratches, complete with magnitudes and depths thereof. You will note any discolorations, paint bubbles, rust, any other damage, etc. Carry a tire tread gauge and measure each one. As you do these things, and I'm sure you've noted this or your manager has told you this, that customers will, more often than not, begin to tell you stories about how such damages came about.

Why do we do this? Yes, in part to devalue the trade. Every bit helps on certain vehicles. If the trade is truly wonderful, we will know this as well.

If there is a concern or viewpoint that exists out there that it doesn't matter if you notice all of these things about their trade, because if another dealership is going to give them more money, we lose, I understand entirely. Normally, it is a valid concern. One of the first rules I developed as a used car manager was not to lose a deal because I'm right. But, by completing this activity and doing it well and convincingly, you will certainly make the customer believe that there might be a similar inspection coming from any facility that just threw out a number. Here is the good news: the tactics you will be provided with here shortly virtually eliminate that obstacle.

One additional thing you can do to help your manager is to check if there are any lights on, i.e.: ABS, check engine, this sort of thing. I know it surprises you as much as it does me how many customers expect top dollar for a trade-in that has obvious issues. But they do and will continue to do so. Understand the human ability for rationalization. You and I have done it. Perhaps we still do to certain degrees and in specific instances. The important part here is to not allow the customer to lose face by maintaining an empathetic and understanding demeanor and an even tone when going over the trade. Professionalism (we will mention this a lot) is the key and it must always be projected.

Now, before we move on to specific concerns, let us discuss a strategy that has worked well for many stores. Again, if yours is not one that uses this, it is not a major item. Many facilities have been using a range on the trade-in. It is extremely effective, in that, no manager has driven the vehicle and it leaves that activity to produce a final number. This is a great tool for leaving the door open and protecting the trust you have developed.

You come back from your manager with a range and present it to your customer like this:

"Based on the information we've shared, all of the sources and the market place have ranged your vehicle's value to be between $_____ and $_____. Shall I have my manager drive the unit so we can continue with the paperwork?"

Believe me, this is where any concerns will arise. And this is what we want. Remember, it's better to get the objections and concerns out so we are able to counter them and close. But, as we've mentioned before and will again, we have to set one another up for success.

I remember a time I was watching one of our customers follow one of our consultants down the hallway, heading back to his desk probably to talk more about the car, and almost as an aside, the customer asked, "How're you guys on trades?" This caught the consultant a little by surprise and he began to tell the customer quite a bit more than he needed to, things like: "Well, that depends on condition, mileage, equipment. Y'know... We'll make some calls if it's not something we stock. And, of course, it depends on what car yer on..."

Now I was the one shaking my head. Again, the consultant was caught by surprise. That was my fault and I had to prepare my team better than I had. But, this was just too much information and we have to watch this throughout the sales process. Less is generally better.

Of course, I am certainly a proponent of communicating with your customer, but I am convinced that full disclosure has a place - and it's not at the beginning. And it should not imply in any way to the customer that we are not going to give them anything for their trade. It doesn't make sense.

So as I told my consultant when we talked about the situation a bit later, the only thing you need to say when a customer asks you that question is: **"Every dollar it's worth and probably a little more."**

John says, "How much will you give me for my trade?"

You respond **"Well, John, every dollar it's worth and probably a little more!"**

John says, "It all depends on my trade."

You say, **"Well you'll be happy to know that we'll give you every dollar it's worth and probably a little more."**

I think the picture is clear. This statement is designed to temporarily, if nothing else, bolster the customers' confidence in us and take the focus off of the trade-in until the proper time.

So, what do we do when the proper time comes?

We will communicate with our customer; let him/her know what we're going to do, then ask permission. As expressed before, the transition goes like this:

"That's the easiest (or simplest) part of the entire process (my job). What I'd like to do now is gather as much information about your vehicle as I can. We will then utilize all the sources and market data available to us. That way, you will be provided with the highest available dollar for your trade-in. Is that all right (OK) with you?"

This will put your customers at ease. You will then begin gathering the information *with* your customer and properly and *completely* filling out the appraisal form.

Now I've heard several ways that one might present the trade evaluation. And, as stated earlier, we will go over everything individually before we talk about combining them for those of us who use a four-square or a modified version. Just as with anything else, and as you all know by now, I'm into using effective methods and word tracks each and every time, no matter what the perception might be. What I mean by this is that it should make no difference whether you are presenting an $8,000 appraisal to someone who wants $12,000 for it, or to someone who expects $800 and receives $1,200. The difference will be in the response of your customer. One will be thrilled, perhaps. *Though if an adequate interview had been done and we had an idea of the customers' expectations, our gross profit should benefit.* The other customer, who had exaggerated expectations, will require some skillful countering word tracks and some feigned indifference. In short, be ready to use the Technique repeatedly until you can help your customers understand their situation and why it's still a wonderful opportunity for them to trade.

So, how do we present the appraisal sheet? One thing we should avoid is holding the numbers to our chests or somehow keeping them concealed until we have "explained" them. This does nothing but make it seem as if we are hiding something. It rapidly decreases trust and comfort. The idea that the customer will not listen to us and will only focus on the numbers if they are laid before them might only be true for a moment. And even so, we would rather have this lack of attention for a short time than to risk our level of trust for even a second.

What we will do then, is lay the sheet down in front of our customers, and, again, say the following:

"Based on the information we've shared, all of our sources and the market place have ranged your vehicle's value to be between $5,500 and $6,000. Shall I have my manager (buyer, manager) drive the unit so that we can continue with the process?"

You will now get your response. If your customer agrees with the numbers, have your manager drive the trade-in and then continue to present the payments or difference or go over the four-square (we'll do some actual presentations in the Putting It All Together Chapter) and write the deal. Again, we are separating the steps for those of us who do not present payments or totals dollars at the same time. This will also come in handy if you are placed in the situation of having to focus solely on the trade, at least initially.

If your customer does not agree with the value, you will see one of the following reactions: 1) the customer will voice their concerns and objections 2) the customer will remain in a stunned silence 3) the customer will rise up and begin to leave you.

If the customer remains in stunned silence, we have a choice to make. Remember the old adage that whoever speaks first loses? Well, there might be some truth to this, but we all have certainly closed sales being the first to break the silence. Also, the customer may be silent, but if there are heads shaking, there is communication. If they are shaking their heads, they're speaking. We might not know what they're saying, but they're speaking. This was brought to my attention by a shrewd consultant who countered my claim that if a customer is shaking their head, they are saying "no," by giving me an example of when this was not the case. He had remained as silent as his customer when the gentleman began shaking his head from side to side for a moment, then turned his wife and said, "You see, honey. I knew they were giving me too little for this at the other place." This response was certainly a rarity and I stood corrected. Although, we should understand that this is something that doesn't come up often and would not be changed for the worse if a solid word track was used.

What if the customer says "That's not enough for my trade!" or something similar?

The most initially effective counter to this, particularly with any employee pricing programs or low interest programs available, is this:

"The reason your trade is worth what it is, is the very same reason you can buy ours for what you can."

If you remember from the first part of this program, one of our major goals is to have one of two responses: "I understand" or "What do you mean?"

The customer says "I understand" and you close "Shall we continue with the paperwork then?"

If the customer says "What do you mean?" then you utilize third party examples to reinforce the number and use the Technique to close the sale.

There are many more objections and concerns, and we will cover them in just a bit, along with other items and reactions that might occur.

Let's briefly discuss what to do if the customer immediately rises and begins to leave. First of all, I have found that this doesn't really happen very often either. Secondly, why are they doing this? Well, they might truly feel insulted. It might be that they have been taught to do this in order to get more money for their trade-in. Either way, it does bring up this point: why not go against what was said earlier, with the example of the sales consultant taken by surprise, and tell these people in advance how we are going to come to their trade figure. Well, we did that already by mentioning sources and market data. We simply chose not to explain to them in advance why the trade will be lower than they expect. It might very well *not* be lower. The customer needs to go in confident as well. Anyway, back the question: What to do?

The customers will probably accompany their actions with some dialogue such as: "Forget it. Let's go!" or "That's insulting! I'm outta here!" or "You must think we're nuts!" or some other such confidence-building phraseology.

Your response, as in the first part of the book when someone threatened to leave over price, is a simple **"Why do you say this?"** or **"Why would you say that, John?"** The key is to remain calm. If they respond, you have your opening. If not, and they continue to pack up and leave, you must be quick and again calm, **"Folks, I would hate to have a misconception cost you a lot of money. Before you go, let me show you how we can save you that money."** A last ditch effort that is more aggressive may be used, particularly if you have developed a high level of rapport. **"John, Judy, I have just spent a bit of time with you folks. It would be a great courtesy for you to give me a minute or two more. I would be grateful for that."** This one has worked well many times. Have confidence and use these words.

What we will do next is look into specific concerns or objections in detail, one at a time. . .

We'll begin with the most common one, the concern we just touched upon.

1. That's not enough for my trade.

    a. **"The reason your trade is worth what it is, is the very same reason you can buy ours for what you can."**

This counter is the easiest to remember and, interestingly enough, it might very well provide the highest impact if delivered properly. This can be used most effectively on new vehicle purchases and particularly when you are taking in a relatively recent model year. Vehicles always take the biggest loss during the first year, and it is a pretty simple matter to use this to your advantage. So if the customer asks you the golden "What do you mean?" how can you respond? On a new vehicle, you explain that along with the great pricing from the factory and the current incentives or discounts or whatever, your brand new vehicle is selling for such a low dollar that the trade-in is in turn slightly affected by this. Explain that the market is tied together like this, always has been. The good news is that the value they receive on the vehicle they are purchasing is far greater than the lesser effect had on the trade-in.

> b. **"The reason your trade is worth what it is, is the very same reason you can buy a 2013 Impala for $13,000 when the vehicle listed for more than $24,000 new only months ago. The two are related. The market is tied together like this."**

This response can be used both in new and used situations. It is similar to the first, but it actually provides a specific example, perhaps a vehicle you have in your own inventory. One major obstacle you might run into is if they are trading a vehicle like one they have seen on your lot for a higher dollar, sometimes quite a bit higher. In reality, this happens in far less instances than one might think. Usually, there are some key differences between the two such as condition or mileage. If there are not, you simply have to try to make the customer understand that there are reconditioning and/or certification costs involved, and that you, as a retail facility, are required to average a certain profit margin on pre-owned vehicles. It is worth what it will run through the auction for, or what you can buy a similar vehicle for and prepare for resale. The one on the lot might also be an aged unit that you are having trouble moving, one that is scheduled for wholesale and therefore a loss. You also can relate to the customer that by taking a trade into the inventory, you are accepting all of the risk that goes along with it, that being the possibility that it does not sell and must be wholesaled for a loss. And guess what? The customer probably doesn't care too much about all of this, but your job is to make them understand the simple truths of the matter and convince them that this is what their vehicle will bring everywhere. Again, thank goodness this situation is rare.

> c. **If nothing owed: "Not a problem. Let's continue with the paperwork on your new vehicle and please take all the time you need to sell your trade."**

This one is particularly handy if you have a buyer who is less than receptive to the majority of your statements. In this case, the customer might seem angry and short. If you respond in this way with a smile and a confidence that portrays a commonness of sorts - that you see this all of the time – you certainly might surprise yourself with an immediate close. If it does not come quickly, you should definitely commend your customer on the wonderful position they are in and indeed how rare such a situation is. And then try to close again. If this is unsuccessful, you can use a reverse application of **9b** in this section.

"Please understand that more and more people are purchasing from retail facilities these days because they want the things that private sellers just can't offer. Things like an inspected vehicle, a vehicle backed by a manufacturer, a warranty or extended service plan option, financing options or a place for you to address your concerns. And independent sellers generally don't take trade-ins."

Once this is said, try to close again. *Never forget to ask for the business.*

Now I can almost hear the Used Car Managers sighing or grunting, "How can we give up the trade so quickly?" Well, we're really not. If the trade is a desirable unit, the manager should have plenty of time to see if it's worth the while to go after it once the new unit is sold.

2. Kelley Blue Book says my trade is worth $_____ more.

   a. **"Kelley Blue Book is a source, maybe the most popular, but there are others, too. And if they were all accurate, they wouldn't differ as much as they do. And they do, don't they?"**

What this does for you is to create the idea that the internet is wrong. You read this correctly. Don't be too shocked. Well, the fact of the matter is that the sources available on the internet really have no clue as to the ebbs and flows of various marketplaces. Unfortunately, many of our customers take it as gospel, even though they had to search for the highest value and then, of course, chose to believe that particular source. It may, in fact, be Kelley Blue Book or some other source – they're interchangeable in this example. We clearly mentioned this mis-information that makes our jobs even more difficult. So, in this case, our responsibility is to throw a shadow of doubt upon their accuracy and help the customer understand that auction reports, along with independent buyers, other new car dealerships, and/or the marketplace in general would be where the real dollars come from.

      b.   **"If Kelley Blue Book were 100% accurate, we would be inclined to raise the prices of most of our used cars."**

This is an extremely strong response because in most cases (you might have to pick and choose based on the inconsistencies of the internet sources) you can show your customers this very fact. Depending on the unit and how it happens to be priced, you should be fine. If your dealership has the practice of using Kelley Blue Book's extremely liberal retail pricing, you will be in a great position if your customer is committed to using this comparison. In a high percentage of cases, you will be able to earn yourself a pretty healthy gross profit.

3.   The dealer down the street is offering _____.

      a.   **"With this they have also given you a total difference figure? And what was that dollar?**

This is most effective with new vehicles, particularly if it happens to be the same make and model offered by a competitor. The idea is to help the customer see the deal as a whole. Also, it helps you break down the deal and discover exactly where the dollars are coming from (whether the trade allowance includes discount and/or incentives – total trade allowance). If the customer does not have a total dollar or any form of a worksheet available, the actual value given to the trade cannot be known. This is made clear to the guest and, hopefully, we can dig deeper and build more value in our deal.

> b. **"Please keep in mind that the other dealership might be asking equal or more money for a lesser or more undesirable vehicle."**

What this counter does is help the customer understand or remember that the prices they might have seen are perhaps too high for the unit they are considering elsewhere, and that a *higher trade-in allowance does not always guarantee a better buy.* In fact, you can use those very words. I have often used the follow-up, "If such is the case, I'm a bit surprised they didn't offer more." Another key effect that this will have is to nullify any bluff. But, your response must be on time, no delay. Make sure you say this calmly and with an understanding smile. This particular response and any follow-up are strongly reinforced by using a third-party example as described in the Technique. This example is on a pre-owned off-brand. "Why just the other day (just last week, not too long ago) I had a gentlemen in who had a similar experience. He mentioned that it was true that the other facility was asking $2,000 more for a vehicle with higher mileage and not in as nice a condition. They couldn't give him enough for his trade to make it worth his while. He took delivery of our Passat that very day." Please remember to use third-party examples whenever you can. They create just a ton of credibility. After all, it's not you trying to convince your customer of anything. It's simply a fact.

On a new vehicle, the third-party example can be just as effective. "Just last week a young couple had a similar concern until they realized that the total dollars paid on the other unit would be quite a bit higher for far less equipment. Even with the perceived higher trade-in, the value for our vehicle was so much greater that they bought it that day."

Another counter involves the same idea that the other dealership is asking too much for a lesser vehicle.

    c. **"If they are asking a bit more, then they utilize any extra profit margin as they see fit. Generally in the trade to make the 'deal' seem better than it is."**

What this one does is place the idea that there is indeed more margin in other makes and models without actually making that claim. It makes it easy for us to elaborate on the point once the seed is planted. But don't lose sight that this is also a stand-alone, like the others, from which we are able to close.

    d. **"Please, don't allow a misconception to cost you money."**

This is a catch-all for many situations and seems to generate the "What do you mean?" or at least a quizzical expression more often than not. This statement makes people think. It makes them stop (in most cases) to consider what they might be missing. It helps you keep them on the hook, so to speak.

So what might the misconceptions be? The first is that just because you are seeing more for your trade, you are getting a better buy. As we know, this just isn't always the case. What really matters is what you are getting for your hard-earned dollar. We have to make our customer see this. Another misconception is that the other facility is really putting that much into the trade-in. Aside from using comparisons, like Kelley Blue Book or other internet sources, when they benefit you, it can be effective to point out that on most trades everyone uses the same sources. If the customer visits four dealerships in the area, chances are that the same independent buyers (wholesalers, if you use them) are being called. You can let your customers know this and the only difference is, again, how the other facility chooses to use its added mark-up.

If, in fact, this is not a bluff, your quick, confident responses will buy you some gross with just a bit of doubt being planted. And, if this is the case, you will now be able to work on stealing the business away because your customer will tell you what you are up against. In such a situation, you can frankly ask which vehicle they truly prefer and with which establishment they wish to do business.

4. I know for a fact that my trade is worth _____.

a. "And I would agree with you, perhaps though from a retail perspective. And should you wish to attempt to sell it yourself, you might very well ask that figure to start."

The power in this one is that you fully agree with your customer right away, and then explain a condition. From this, you can again use a form of **9b** about how difficult it is for private owners to receive a true retail price. "More and more wish to purchase from a retail facility because they offer an inspected vehicle, a vehicle backed by a manufacturer, any warranty or extended service plan options, financing options or a place for you to address your concerns. Private owners do not."

b. "Please keep in mind that these other vehicles are sitting for those prices, not selling. You might see what others are asking, but what they actually receive is not reported."

If your customers mention that they have seen the same vehicle as their trade on another lot, in the paper, or over the internet for a certain dollar, you will now be able to respond quickly and strongly with this one. For greatest impact, as with all others, this should be used with the Technique. Third-party examples and pull-back or retreat statements are vital to properly setting up the close. There will continue to be more specific examples of how some of these counters work within the Technique as we move forward in the book.

5. "I just think so," or "I think my trade is worth _____."

    a. "Well, John, we certainly couldn't and wouldn't over-charge a friend or family member of yours on a fine, pre-owned vehicle just because someone 'thought' their trade was worth more. It's not fair (to them or any other customer."

We go back to explaining how important this customer is to you and how you do need referrals to friends and family to come in and buy from you.

    b. "I can't tell you how many times a bank will come back and say the balance is too high for the vehicle. It's not because the margin is too high, it's because the market can change so quickly. Now these folks can't buy the vehicle they want..."

6. My bank/credit union says my trade is worth _____.

    a. "I have no doubt. In fact, they use some of the very same sources that we do. But, please keep in mind that it is difficult for the bank to come up with an accurate number with all of the inconsistencies in these sources. That is why we utilize market reports and independent buyers as well."

This concern is a common one, so please take heed of this counter. Again, you do not deny that the bank has stated such a value, you agree that they use similar sources, but you confidently present why it is that your number is accurate and real and more than sufficient.

      b. **"These things will provide more accurate information based on regional differences and/or current incentives. And please understand that because of the great way we do business, we are always striving to obtain the highest value possible for your trade."**

Again, this explains a little about how and why the trade value came in as it did. It also reinforces that we are obligated to do whatever we can to give them the highest value possible. Also, without seeming too old-school, it doesn't hurt to mention that the bank or credit union will not buy the trade-in and that they are receiving as much or more than they would if they were able to sell their vehicle at auction. There is an ambiguity too, in that, the bank might give one value going in that would make it impossible for them to finance it on the retail side without an enormous amount of money down. Tough situation for the retailer and the customer.

7. That's insulting! Let's get/I'm outta here!

      a. **"Why would you say this?"**

Recall the part in the beginning of this chapter.

8. Can I have a little more than that?

    a. **"I certainly appreciate you asking. Please understand that we try very hard to give you every dollar your vehicle is worth and probably a bit more. And we certainly have here."**

This is a question that is asked very rarely by a type "A", crabby, or highly disappointed customer. Most often it is asked by a very nice, receptive, timid or younger person, or, stereotypically, by the little old lady. They show a moderate level of understanding or they just want a little more to feel better about their purchase. They generally never specify exactly just how much more would do the trick. Our job is to make them feel comfortable and believe that they have received every dollar and more because they deserve it. And, don't forget the warm fuzzies. Tell them how important they are to us and why.

9. Give me _____ more and we have a deal.

    a. **"Actually, you are already getting $_____ because of the tax savings (more effective with higher dollar trades). It's a benefit of trading."**

This is an old one. It's simply a tax savings counter. Just take the value of the trade-in, multiply it by your tax rate and explain that it's an added bonus, similar to receiving that dollar amount for the trade. Again, more effective with higher value trades, of course. The key, as with anything else, is to sound confident as though this bit of information should be enough to make the customer buy now.

10. You're giving me wholesale for mine and you want retail for yours!

   a. **"Well, that's what we do. We are a retail facility. In reality, though, you are only paying a modest profit as compared to others and reconditioning (in the case of pre-owned)."**

   This particular counter actually had its birth from sheer frustration. I overheard one of my fine sales consultants, Jay Dowthard, exclaim this out of exasperation after trying several other counters and not getting anywhere. I immediately found the brilliance in its simplicity. He closed the deal. Then we talked about it, embellished it, and decided that it would be even more effective without the excess emotion – just have fun. I used it a month later with another couple who had already had their vehicle ranged on a prior date and came back trying for more (quite a bit as I remember). The husband used this exact objection, "You're giving me wholesale for mine and you want retail for yours." I smiled and said "Henry, that's what we do! We're a retail facility." The wife got a little kick out of that. Of course I added, "Remember when I said that the reason yours is worth what it is, is the very same reason you can buy ours for what you can? You can see the relationship. Let's continue with the paperwork." Done deal. It won't always work, but you have to try. If nothing else, it saves you gross.

b. "Please understand that, as a retail facility, we need to do things that way. Private sellers do not offer an inspected vehicle, a vehicle backed by a manufacturer, any warranty or extended service plan options, financing options or a place for you to address your concerns. And they certainly will not take trade-ins."

This is the counter to which we have referred a couple of different times already. It's pretty straight-forward. This explains our need to take in the trades at wholesale – to provide our retail customers, like themselves, with the greatest value and options. And it explains why we ask a certain price for our retail units. This transitions nicely into the next counter...

c. "Yes, you are receiving wholesale. The secret is that *all* retail facilities put wholesale values into the trade-ins. You are, on the other hand, getting more for your dollar on this vehicle. The value you receive is far better here."

The idea here is to again make your customer realize that trade-in values are determined in a similar manner everywhere they might shop. There is no distinction. The variation is in the pricing and the total difference of dollars, where we always come out on top. Granted, there is the temptation from time to time to confront your customer and ask them point blank if they are buying a trade allowance or a vehicle. Avoid this direct approach if you can. Better to use a third-party example (can you tell I love these things?). "Y'know, John, just the other day, I had someone so concerned about trade-in value that he nearly spent $1,500 more on a similar unit because that was all he was focused upon. He caught it, luckily, and purchased our unit – the one that had the far lower total difference in dollars." While this is powerful, don't forget to use value whenever possible.

11. You'll just put my trade out for _____!

      a. "Perhaps, but we assume all of the risk as well."

      Many times the customer suggests that you will put their trade-in out for far more than you really would. In such a case, be honest. "We'd actually probably put this on the lot for about $_____ ." Then add, "But even there we are assuming all of the risk." This counter attracts the response, or one similar to, "What do you mean?" with the best of them. If this is the circumstance, you are welcome to educate the customer about a 60-day aged policy or the importance of turning the inventory quickly. Values continue to drop - this is your risk. You will have added to the cost of the unit with reconditioning, clean-ups, other maintenance; and if it does not sell right away, the cost continues to rise. If the vehicle does not sell for some reason, as many do not, you must wholesale it at a loss. True, they probably don't care, but the point has been made. They might come back, "But they're giving me $_____ down the street." You revert to counter number three. It works really well. And, of course, use the Technique.

12. You're going to make _____ on my trade, cut your profit and give me _____.

> **a. "Perhaps. But were we certain of the profit to be made or were we certain of reconditioning costs, we would happily increase or decrease the actual cash value of your trade. Because no dealership knows these things for sure, everyone uses similar means to evaluate a trade. Everyone."**

This is, once again, designed to drive home that every dealership looks at trade-ins the same way. Of course, because of the way we do business, we give them every dollar it's worth and probably a little more – don't we? You might want to explain why your facility is able to put a little more in trades: volume, it's our brand, strong used vehicle department, the customer is very important to us (so is the repeat and referral business) etc. Continue to build value with warm fuzzies and positive-value statements.

> **b. "You really get pretty much the same appraisal no matter where you go. The only thing to consider is the value and difference."**

"What do you mean?" is again a common response, along with "I don't believe that!" Either way, you are set. Are you beginning to see the cycle? With the former, and, of course, golden response, you use the Technique with third-party examples. With the latter, you set up the valuable, "Why would you say this?"

By now, it's surely pretty clear that this is a lot of material. It will take time to master. But, when you do, think about the time saved by not having to call in a manager right away, think about the deals saved, think about the potential gross saved. It's truly amazing what can be accomplished. This is a sport and these are, in all reality, your skills. The better you become, the higher your closing percentages and gross will grow - your CSI as well.

13. I have to have what I owe.

   a. **"I can certainly appreciate that. Every day we see people who owe more than their vehicle is worth. If they are able, they still purchase ours when they understand that the two values are completely unrelated." (Go to payment or difference)**

This is a wonderful, if not preliminary counter. Again – smile and be confident in appearance and tone as if you fully expected this response. If your customers are unable to grasp the meaning of this, follow with this on a new vehicle:

   b. **"You are actually in a position better than most. Further, the manufacturer understands this and has provided you the means through incentives to go ahead and upgrade your vehicle anyway."**

This counter should allow you to sell the value of the unit as well as the incentives, whether it be cash or finance rate (not so much at this time, I know). Show them what they are able to do. Write them up, get them payments or a difference. Don't let them go. Make the customer understand that they are not alone; in fact, they are in a great position to buy what they want to buy this time (see payments). After all, they want to trade for a reason.

14.   I'll get more if I sell it myself.

> a. **"I believe you would if you were able to sell it. And, by all means, please do so if you like. I will help if I can. Please understand though that more people are purchasing from retail facilities now for very simple reasons. Private sellers cannot offer an inspected vehicle, they cannot offer warranties or extended service plan options, they cannot offer financing options, and the only person to talk to if anything goes wrong is you."**

This is powerful, in that, you agree with them and then offer to help. They are probably expecting something quite a bit different: that being confrontation – "You can't possibly get that for your vehicle!" As a relief to your used car manager, you are indeed attempting to bring in the trade.

> b. **If nothing owed – go to 1c.**

There is nothing wrong with this response if you see no alternative and are looking for a quick close (our goal, of course.) With practice, the sequencing of these word tracks will become a part of you and you will be smoother than silk no matter what is thrown your way.

>   c.   **If upside down: "How will you secure the title if you do not receive what you owe?"**

What this is designed to do is make them understand that, for instance, if the trade is appraised at $10,000 and the customer still owes $15,000 and they claim that they can sell it for at least $12,000, they will have to come up with $3,000 just to get the title for the buyer. Do they have the three thousand dollars, and, if not, why not just use the incentives and let the manufacturer help buy them out of the vehicle as the incentives are designed to do? (See 12b)

15. I just put $_____ into my vehicle.

>   a.   **"I can appreciate that. Please understand that the buyers who bid these vehicles expect everything to be in relatively good order. The good news is, you're trading it and you won't have to put any more dollars into it."**

This is a great opportunity to show the customer that now is indeed the perfect time to get out of the unit. We will talk about the maintenance counter later in the book when we discuss payments. Now, I understand that if the customer is trading in an old $300 piece, this one might be difficult. But, this is where a third-party example will help them understand that it's still a $300 car with everything working.

"John, just the other day I had someone voice very similar frustrations. He ultimately realized that a 10 year-old vehicle with 130,000 miles is extremely suspect to a potential buyer. And that was why he was looking to upgrade."

If this doesn't get it done... Technique.

16.   If that's all you're going to give me, I'll keep it.

   a. **"You have to want the new car more than your trade-in."**

A quick story... A father and mother were in to buy a car for their daughter. Everything went according to plan until the trade appraisal (sound familiar). My consultant had done all the right things. He had complimented the mother and father for taking their valuable time to make sure the daughter was getting a good deal. I was called in to explain the appraisal. Well, true to consistency that is all important, I echoed everything my consultant had told them. The mother responded with the concern, "If that's all you're going to give us, we'll keep it." I responded immediately. "That is entirely your choice. That's the wonderful thing about our store. It's all up to you. You're in control." I continued... "Please understand, you have to want the new car more than your trade-in. But, I imagine that's why you're here." The mother responded, "Okay, we're leaving." The father and daughter did not give the same impression. I said, "As I said, you have to see the value. If you do, continue the paperwork and get this wonderful new vehicle for your daughter. If not, we understand." I looked at the daughter, "What do you think?" I asked. "Mom?" she asked. Now I got up and left. "I'll let you decide," I said, leaving. "Brian, give them some time," I followed. The father replied, "It is the best buy we've seen. Let's do it, honey." And again, done deal. Will this always work? No, of course not. Further, of course I chose a successful example! But, use the Technique and give yourself the best chance every time. The key is to *ask* for the sale.

Chapter In-Review

1. Silent or Active Walkaround

No matter what your management team decides to call this, and if it is part of your sales process, it should be done all of the time. If there is ever a thought in your head that makes you believe another consultant might not be going to this extreme measure, or did not before shooting out a trade figure, lose that thought. You are planting a seed that it might happen again. And this is valuable. If this is not part of your process, abide by the wishes of your management team.

2. Don't "Hope."

I have heard such words out of the mouths of many, many sales consultants. I've said such a thing myself when I was on the floor. "Boy, I hope the trade is worth _____." This is absolutely, 100% okay to think or say IF the intention is to create gross. If it is hoped so that you can make your job easier – stop it! It's time for another mind-set change.

BEYOND THE WALKAROUND

Payments

If your customer is not a true cash buyer and, more than likely, also a difference buyer, you will probably want to offer payment options at the same time you present the trade value. I agree whole-heartedly with the facilities that choose to always present a payment even if the customers claim they are cash buyers. There really is no reason to lose an opportunity if somehow a switch is turned-on and the customer chooses to finance and keep the cash liquid. There are a couple of important reasons for this. One, it gives the customer something other than the trade-in allowance to focus upon. Two, it will bring any payment concerns to light right away.

Giving the customer something else to think about might slow them down a bit naturally. Also, if the payment is low enough or within their budget, the trade value might somehow seem less important – maybe. But you should give yourself every opportunity. Secondly, knowing any payment objections will help you avoid taking time and energy to overcome a plethora of trade value concerns only to find that the customer cannot afford the payment even if you could give them what they wanted for their trade. If this is the case, you will obviously have to focus on payment and attempt to bump them (we'll go over the best way later); or you will try to switch them to another vehicle. A lot of our customers seem to struggle with math now and then – we need to head this off at the pass, if possible.

One of the things we will talk about during this, the payment chapter, will be how to not jump right to rate reduction, trade bumps, extended terms or changing vehicles, as we suggested just moments ago, in order to meet the payment requirement of our customer. That being said, it is true that all of these used, if necessary, will help you close some deals. It's the when and the how that is more important.

A quick note about difference buyers – they are generally easier to close than rate buyers or trade buyers or incentive buyers (not necessarily payment buyers, though), because most of them are looking for the total dollars and what value is represented. If we are able to help them understand the value, we will earn their business.

As with most other things, different facilities will handle the presentation of the payment in different ways. While there might be a few stores which choose not to have sales people discuss payments or certainly not interest rates, the majority will present these things to their customers consistently.

Some might handle the trade-in separately; some might do both at the same time.

While going over the trade by itself keeps our steps on the road to the sale neat, it also opens the door to losing sight of the customers' ultimate goal. That being cash difference or payment.

It has happened often that we have a concern or two over the trade-in value that makes the customer upset enough to avoid purchasing. We, of course, being highly-skilled, eventually overcome these concerns only to find out, as stated earlier, that the payment is too high anyway.

Note: Payments and trade-ins are tied together. As some customers see it: "The more for the trade, the lower the payments and the lower the money down." And they are correct. One important factor – the $500 needed to lower their payment $9 or so a month is too precious to us in relation to the effort necessary to bump the customer the nine dollars.

If all of our customers chose to do things in their true best interest in regard to payments, our jobs would be a lot easier. Unfortunately, the majority of the public, even with the help of the consumer advocates, still does not understand this and wish to take the best course of action when purchasing an item that depreciates as rapidly as an automobile. One would ideally finance for the shortest term possible, with the most down payment they can spare without putting themselves at risk, and take the highest payments they can reasonably afford. But, most do not. And we get it. Budget vs. Income.

Even with a 0% or low interest opportunity, it might be better for your customer to take advantage of the cash incentive, particularly if they plan to pay the vehicle down soon. An example of this is when a woman paid a six percent higher rate and chose the $3,000 cash incentive because she was going to pay the unit off later in the year. This is an opportunity for us to earn extra gross profit. In reality, though, most car buyers have been trained to do just the opposite. They come into our facilities wanting the lowest possible payments, with the least amount of money down, and no matter what the term in a lot of cases.

The majority of our customers are still payment buyers.

It seems as though everyone is advertising low payments. There is a reason for it. They drive certain traffic – in fact, they drive most of it. And ever since the introduction of 0% offered by the factory some years ago, there are a large segment of buyers who look only for 0% – no matter how much they might spend on the car. There are simply a lot of payment buyers out there, and they want those payments to be low. Most of the buying public care very little that taking or making the highest payment they can handle will place them in an equity position far more quickly during the life of the loan. And unfortunately, many of them are not familiar with the principles of basic mathematics. Anyone acquainted with these principles understands that it all comes down to total dollars financed, interest rate, and term. It is our job to educate our customers.

Now, what components make up the total dollars financed or bottom line? This value is represented by price of the vehicle, the trade-in (if applicable), factory cash, and customer cash.

What do we do when we present our payment or payment ranges and we come up against a concern right off the bat – the most common perhaps is that the payment is just too high or more than your customer had budgeted? What would our natural tendencies influence us to do? We did learn a way to begin drilling-down on this concern back in the Preparing For The Purchase Consultation chapter. But, let's say we don't have it down yet. Here's what an untrained consultant might do... If there is a trade present, we could immediately run to our used car manager and beg for more money. And, I'm sure that would make his or her day! We could suggest that they go a longer term or that our wonderful finance manager could get them the lowest rate and thereby reduce the total payment. Of course, that finance manager would not include the options of extended service plans, GAP protection, maintenance, tire and wheel protection, Credit Life and Disability, or other such money making products. This, of course, is not how this will come to pass, except as a last resort and then decided by your sales manager. Please remember that it is your responsibility to set your managers up for success as much as it is theirs for you. To discover what to do before we take to these lengths, we will immediately dive into our basic payment concerns.

One thing to remember is to always be in character, just as with presentation of trade appraisals, when going over payment options. Go in with a smile, good body language, and a positive attitude. Take nothing personally and be surprised by nothing. Your job is to make sure your customers believe that everything is as it should be - business as usual.

Another very telling example of this not being the case was that of a rather high performing consultant. This consultant, who had a bit of a propensity for moodiness from time to time, came into my office one day with an Oh, Crap! look on his face. He then started to chuckle a little, and said "Oh man, I have to be more careful." "What'd you do," I asked. He said he walked up to his customer, a repeat fortunately, and before he could tell her the payment, she asked "What's the matter?" Well, the payment was quite a bit higher that the consultant thought his customer would take, and he displayed it all over his face to the point of bringing about a reaction. The customer ended up taking the unit, but this consultant asked me to help him prepare himself a little better in the future. "Keep reminding me!" he told me. I did. But, he fixed his own problem by being aware and working on it himself.

We are now going to take the most common payment concerns one-at-a-time...

1. That's too high.

    a. **"When you say 'too high,' do you mean too high for this unit or more than you budgeted for your monthly payment?"**

If you have studied the Preparing For The Purchase Consultation chapter of this book, you will remember this counter when used concerning the selling price of the vehicle. If the customer responds that it is too high for the vehicle, you should ask them why they would feel this way or a simple "Why would you say that?" with the complete understanding that you will have to continue to build value in the unit. The customer will tell you that they just think so or that they have seen another vehicle advertised for a lower payment. If it is a competitor, you will use competitive comparisons and utilize the possibility that more money down is required to reach that payment. It is now math entirely, but, if you must, the **"What have you read or heard that drew you to the conclusion that the payment should be less?"** is a good question again.

2. That's $_____ more than where I wanted to be.

This concern does come up a lot, and in deference to the bad English (there's probably a good lot in this book), we'll just take it for what it is and continue. Rather than go right to trade or term or rate . . . Say this:

    a. **"Many of my customers find it easier to find a bit more in their budget now, if at all possible, rather than to settle for something they really don't want, only to discover in a year or two, maybe less, that they purchased a vehicle that they no longer wish to pay for. . . We see it every day and it can cost them thousands."**

Then use The Technique to close immediately. *"Understanding this, shall we continue with the paperwork?"*

Again, many of you will recognize the idea of this counter from that of the price concern introduced in the first part of this book. What it is designed to do is, if nothing else, open the customers' eyes to the benefit of a higher payment. Obviously, people come into the purchase with a limit in mind.

3. I won't go more than 60 months.

    a. **"Please keep in mind that the fact that loans are simple interest these days enables many to extend the term just a bit, knowing that they can pay a little more off later with no penalty."**

This will, hopefully, at least suggest the possibility of going 66 or 72 months or more. This is not something we would like to offer right away, but an extended term, after all else has failed, might be exactly what is necessary to close the deal. Back to setting others up to succeed, an extended term might be what is necessary for the Business Manager to include product. We, as consultants would like to leave this open to him/her. Be that as it may, when discussing this idea, you will want to make it seem as though this is not a major issue, and that it is quite common. And, if it's required or you need a little more reinforcement, explain the simple interest to your customer.

    b. **"The loans are no longer front-loaded, that is to say you don't pay all of your interest due up-front. A payment of just a bit more once in a while will shorten your loan back to sixty months or less quickly over the course of the next few years. But, your minimum payment will remain where you want it to be."**

4. What interest rate are you using?

Of course, we would rather not lock ourselves into an interest rate before we get a call back from the bank. We should understand, though, that other dealerships will quote payments or rates and then hope to "bump" the customer when they take delivery. Depending on the customer's credit rating, we might have to do this as well. Luckily, this should not be your concern. The business manager will handle it in most cases. But we should make it an exception rather than a rule. Well, what if you are asked about these things? Some have tried this:

a. **"We just use a standard factor until we have a call from a bank. Speaking of that, who do you bank through? Chances are we represent them here."**

In all fairness, there are customers who seem more focused on interest rate than they do the price of the vehicle or the trade value. But what this counter is designed to do is to quickly turn the attention away from the rate and toward the deal as a whole. If your customer presses you on the issue, go for a close...

b. **"If everything comes down to rate, why don't we go ahead and fill out a credit application, continue with the other paperwork, and schedule a time for you to pick up your new vehicle?"**

This tactic will almost always bring up any other concerns or objections your customer might have. If it seems a little to forward or abrupt, remember it's all how you say your words. Say them with kindness, empathy, and the matter-of-fact nature will not become an obstacle. If they continue to press, here is one more that should put it to bed…

    c. **"Rest assured that you will not be asked to sign a contract until your rate is disclosed down to the 100th of a percent and your payment to the penny. You have no worries."**

Then move forward and attempt to counter anything else and close the sale. Always ask for the business. This should give you every opportunity to use your knowledge and skill to capture the financing for our store.

5. That interest rate is too high.

Okay, if all goes well, our finance or business manager will be taking care of the interest rate concerns or objections when it comes right down to it. But there will be some instances in some facilities when the sales consultant is dealing with this. It happens often when a worksheet is given that shows an average interest rate of some kind. It can be any rate, but the customer will see it and assume that this is an actual rate quote, which it is not. If you are a salesperson who frequently shows rates, here is a counter for you to use in this case...

    a. **"John, there are many factors that go into arriving at an interest rate. The fact of the matter, however, is that we don't set it. A bank does. The banks we represent, your bank or credit union, whatever. Try to understand that your goal and ours is to secure the best rate for you, and we can."**

Try to move on, as if this is the simple truth of the matter, and that it is no big deal. It happens every day.

6.   Let me check with my credit union/bank.

    a. **"That sounds great! If you are going to your credit union, you must have decided to buy the vehicle. Thank you for your business. Let's continue with the paperwork so that you have everything you need for your approval."**

The key here is to attempt to close. More objections might surface, or, in many cases, your customer will agree and you will have sold a car. If so, you must get them to a business manager or sales manager before the customer leaves. We still must do everything possible to convert them to our financing or, if nothing else, sell that extended service plan or other products. If you do not have a positive response to this, offer this:

    b. **"All interest rates are generally published. Please allow my business manager to quote**

you a payment using your own credit union's rate. If all is well, we can wrap this up right now."

Let's talk about credit unions or banks for a bit more. You certainly do not want people to initially go to their own bank or credit union. In fact, when they let you know this is their intention, you are obligated to let your business manager or manager know. If the business manager decides that it would be in our best interest for the customer to visit his/her credit union, such will be the case. This is rare. If your customers go to their bank or credit union, there is a chance that these institutions will tell them that they are paying too much for the vehicle. They do not have a working knowledge of the car business. Most do not understand or concern themselves with factors such as: demand, reconditioning costs, certification costs, margins, etc. If, somehow, your customer gets one by you and calls to say that their credit union said the vehicle is priced too high, you say this:

"That is just a nice way of them telling you they'd like to see some money down."

The premise here is that the bank or credit union does not want to be the bad guy. Again, you will either be able to close or you will bring up another concern.

If you cannot push past this, please get them to a business manager or manager. Going forward. . .

7. I need my payment to stay the same or less.

Do you recall, for some of us it's more difficult, that kid you sat next to in third or fourth grade math class who continually complained about what he is ever going to use this stuff for? Well, that kid frequently makes his/her way to our dealerships. It's the same kid who grows up to be that guy or gal who thinks that a $25, 000 car can be financed, with no money down, for $250/mth. And, believe me, it's always a tougher situation than it should be. But, no one likes to feel stupid, or be told they're wrong, or anything else that hurts the precious psyche. So how do we handle this? Well, as with anything else, we behave ourselves. We empathize, we keep a kind demeanor and expression about ourselves, and we do everything we can to help the customer save face.

   a. **"It all comes down to basic math. I have found that some folks will be open to pay just a bit more if they are driving something they would rather drive. You have to want the new vehicle more than your trade."**

The major point here to make is that the customer must understand that they must want to pay more for a newer, fresher, nicer, safer, more advanced automobile than the one they are currently driving. In most cases, keeping the payment the same is pretty tough. And although you really shouldn't come right out with this when your customers say they want to keep the payment the same, your thoughts should probably go to the idea that they don't want to upgrade at all. They would rather continue to drive a vehicle in the same condition with the same equipment and advancements that they are driving now. "So, what you're saying is that you'd kinda rather buy another car just like the one you have now?" "No, I'd like something nicer. That's why I'm here." Now, it's up to us to help them understand that buying something better generally costs people more money. Also understand, this might have been headed-off at the pass during a quality interview or needs assessment.

8. I don't have any money to put down.

   a. "I understand. Obviously, the more you can put down the better. A lot of us have resources that we don't think about. Other people, other vehicles, merchandise. In order to get the vehicle you want, perhaps you could do without some other things. It's up to you. What do you think?"

   There has been good success with this idea, the idea that people have sources for funds all around them in some cases: relatives, items they no longer want and would be willing to sell, that savings account no one wants to touch (but we can always put it back later), etc. The goal here is to make your customer realize that down payment is the best way to go and sometimes very necessary.

9. If you can get the payment down to _____, I'll take the vehicle.

   a. "Please keep in mind that the payment is based on math. If it is just a bit more than you

**would like, put a little more money down, or
consider paying up for a vehicle you really
want. Please buy what you would like to
buy." See #2 above.**

This one is pretty self-explanatory, but what should
be gone over before we close this section are a couple of
traditional counters or ideas that should really be in the
arsenal of all salespeople. Those would be the gas mileage
or maintenance arguments (again, some call these closes,
but they're actually counters).

Prepare for the maintenance argument by asking
your customer what repairs have been recently done to
his/her trade-in – again, follow the instructions of your
sales managers on this, and everything else for that
matter. Right, wrong, or not, it's always wise to follow the
processes and rules laid down by your store. Anyway, the
simple way to handle this is to follow a payment concern
with a "So, what you're saying is that if you were able to
find another $50 a month in your budget, you'd take the
new car?" With luck, they will say "yes," then you point
out that they had just done $1,200 in repairs over the last
year and that they would have had $100 month extra had
they had this new or newer vehicle. Same with the gas
mileage... If it is true that they have a potential to save a
certain amount every month because of the efficiency of
the new vehicle, they would do well to buy it now and
start enjoying it.

<u>Leasing</u>

Although the section on payments has virtually come to a close, I believe it is appropriate to devote a bit of time to leases. Many, many high-volume facilities do a great business with leases. Because of the customer retention capacity (great for the consultant and the dealership – manufacturer, too), the short turn-around, the ability to capture fantastic one-owner trade-ins, leases are wonderful. Please defer to your management staff and present these as recommended.

If you have had the good fortune to have been around the business for twenty years or better, you are familiar with the big push for leasing that took place at the turn of the nineties (late eighties, early nineties) when so many experts predicted that 90% of all automobiles would be leased by 1998. While many dealerships across the country bought into this and have done very well with leasing, it never even approached that highly aggressive percentage and it doesn't seem it ever will. In fact, the ridiculously high residual values and low money factors led to many job losses across the banking industry. And this is certainly not the place to go into close-ended vs. open-ended leases. That would be a history lesson; one that, unlike most, has been studied and heeded. At any rate, for many new vehicles, there is still a large opportunity for leases.

Now, for those of you who remember the "Better Way" or the "Half-a-Car" programs that encouraged the prospective lessee to pay only for the part of the car they wish to use – the best part of the life of the automobile, the portion under warrantee, we do recall that leasing does have its benefits. But there are differing mind-sets throughout the public.

The fact of the matter is that no one, since the advent of the close-ended lease has been "screwed" by a lease. They simply were not communicated the terms and consequences of breaking these terms, or they didn't understand, or they chose not to be accountable for their actions. It's the same for finance customers... They were "screwed" because they chose a long term with no money down on a severely depreciating product (item) and now it's the dealerships fault. Leasing is not really that much different from conventional purchase or financing. One does, however, as was taught in the "Better Way" and "Half-a-Car" or any other lease training available, truly have three options: Walk away, purchase, or trade (if able). These are good things.

What about the people who want to have something when they trade? They, of course, mean negative equity? If no down payment, or a minimal one, was made, the customer is worse off than otherwise. Further, these customers do not own the vehicle when they finance. How often have we heard the flippant remark: "Well, you'll learn who really owns it when you miss a payment or two!" This is true.

You really own nothing more than the opportunity to owe more than the vehicle is worth, particularly, again, if you chose to put little down, finance for a long term and have the yearning to trade within a two or three-year cycle. And this is really no fun.

In truth, you can, as a customer, drive a little more vehicle than you could normally afford with a lease over a standard finance contract. You will, in most cases, drive a vehicle during a warranty period, avoiding any major repair costs. You will be in a cycle that allows you to get into a new car every 2-3 years rather than 4-5 years. But, be sure to remind your customers that this is the goal. Many lessees pay a bit more every month to allow this unusually short trade cycle and the ability to drive a vehicle that is always in warranty.

What about the naysayers...? Those who say that they were "screwed" by driving too many miles, or who were charged for excess damage? You must explain to your customer that there is no difference.

If they have financed the unit and have driven too many miles, what happens? It costs them on trade-in. If they have damage and have chosen not to repair it, what happens? It costs them on trade-in. There is no difference. Pay now or pay later.

Leasing is a wonderful opportunity for a salesperson to convert people to short-term trade cycles. This has always been the idea. Use it if you have the programs available. And yes, it can provide customers with lower payment options, particularly with the availability of 48 and, yes, 60 month leases. These are not recommended for customer retention or satisfaction. I encourage you to communicate with your customer. Tell them what is involved. With your skill, you will still sell the vehicle, but you will maintain a relationship that will foster referrals and repeat business. Communication is the most important thing. Always let them know terms and consequences. The excitement will sell the vehicle. Yes, there will be those who refuse to accept responsibility. In the others, you will have earned their trust and hopefully the repeat business.

Leases, when available and viable, should always be offered with all payment options. In closing this section, I would make clear that all of the great ideas presented during the trade-in and payments chapters are only as good as the salesperson delivering them. Again, practice is a must. Anticipate what your customer might say or do and then respond as you have trained. You'll be amazed at the results.

Chapter In-Review

1. **Remember The Following Statement (and how much it means to you and the store):**

   The $500 needed to lower the customer's payment $9 or so a month is too precious to us in relation to the effort necessary to bump the customer the nine dollars.

2. **PLEASE... Do Not Fear Interest Rate Questions!**

   I cannot tell you how many times I have had to go over interest rate concerns in meetings. I cannot tell you how many times I've had to go over them after I have gone over them several times. It seems that this is a real catching point with most of us. And I do understand that we certainly have interest rate buyers. 4C should be a savior for you:

   "Rest assured that you will not be asked to sign a contract until your rate is disclosed down to the 100th of a percent and your payment to the penny. You have no worries."

BEYOND THE WALKAROUND

Putting It All Together

Delivering Your Words

In this section of Putting It All Together, we are going to talk a little about rate, inflection, tone, and expression. What are they? Why are they important? But, first, here are the traditional meanings for these things...

Rate: A certain amount of one thing, as speed, considered in relation to a unit of another, as time.

Inflection: modulation of the voice; the change in the form of a word to express grammatical or syntactic relations, as of case or number; *alteration of pitch or tone of the voice, perhaps to emphasize;* a particular vocal quality that indicates some emotion or feeling.

Tone: any sound considered with reference to its quality, pitch, etc.; a tint or shade of color; *a particular vocal quality that indicates some emotion or feeling.*

Expression: a person's facial appearance, indicating feeling.

There are various definitions for these things, but we are going to break them down the following way: Rate will be how fast or slow you speak; Inflection will be how you alter your voice in the attempt to emphasize an idea or point; Tone will be the vocal quality that indicates some emotion or feeling; and Expression will be, quite simply, how that face of yours looks when you are with your customers.

All of these things must be given attention in order to provide the most effective use of your word tracks.

The *rate* of your speech is very important. Why is this an issue? Shouldn't it be relatively easy to control your rate of speech? Maybe. But for most it is difficult. And this is why practice is so necessary. Think about what would cause us to speak far too quickly. The customer has just asked us a question or created an obstacle and we want to get by it as quickly as possible. We want to spew out as much information as we can in order to overcome their point or emphasize ours. And we want to do it now. We feel compelled not to give our customers a word in edgewise. This is particularly true as our knowledge increases. We know so much more than our customers, we know we can make them understand, but we don't realize that we cannot hit them with consecutive points and create a barrage effect. The term "fast-talker" didn't just pop into our vernacular for the heck of it. People are less likely to trust people who speak too quickly. It seems too much like something is trying to be slipped by them. Excitement also plays a major role. A particular salesman was developing some of these word tracks and committed them to memory, but he was so excited when someone gave him an opportunity to use them that he rushed them out. He responded lightning fast. What he was doing in a sense was showing off. And people can pick up on this. If you're too fast with the response, you are one of those who have an answer for everything. Now, here's a simple truth: you *do* want to have an answer for everything, but it must be metered and precise and, most difficultly, natural sounding. What if you speed through something as simple as part of our welcome and qualification? Read all of these to yourself, out loud and as quickly as you are able.

"Pleasure to meet you. Thank you for choosing to spend some time with us today.

Well, _____, have you been here before. Have you purchased a vehicle (bought a car) here before?"

It sounds strange and I am sure that none of us would do this intentionally, but imagine if you overcame a concern just as quickly and consecutively. Do the same as before with the following counters:

"Dealer XYZ will give me $1000 off for just walking in the door. Will you?"

"Please don't allow a misconception to prevent you from saving money."

"If a vehicle is priced correctly, no major discount should be necessary."

"Either they, themselves, believe the price is too high or the vehicle is not quite right somehow."

"Unfortunately, it seems that they are struggling with the value of their vehicle for some reason."

Whew!! Pretty annoying, overbearing, and altogether ineffective. And I think you get my point.

On the other extreme, if you speak too slowly, your customer will lose interest and not hear your words, the same as if you spoke too rapidly to be understood. In short, you will bore them to death. This, speaking too slowly, does not occur much for us in this business, but it is still something to be aware of. Being tired or distracted are common causes of this. So get enough rest and always maintain focus.

Inflection is extremely important, too. You will repeat and listen to the word tracks and decide if your inflection is effective and natural sounding, or if it sounds canned or like you are reciting poetry. It is powerful to emphasize certain words, but be careful because inflection and tone, which we will briefly touch on in a bit, can actually alter the meaning of your words. Any of you prone to or familiar with sarcasm know this to be true. But what else? Let's look at a simple qualifying question; "What would you like to accomplish today?" If I emphasize the word "today," and say it again, "What would you like to accomplish *today*?" the question takes on a different meaning. It also increases pressure and decreases comfort. This might be true for everything we say. I know this might seem trivial and the example is certainly basic, but the idea has been made clear. And with this one in particular, the placement is important. While it is rather non-threatening with no sarcasm near the beginning or welcome, it can be taken far differently at the end of a presentation or write-up. The customer says "I have to think about it" or "Thank you for your time," and you say "John, what did you come here to accomplish today?" You might as well throw "what on earth" in there somewhere. There can be huge differences in meaning with placement as well as with inflection.

Another very important aspect of how we deliver our word tracks is *tone*. Your tone can express a world of feeling. Often, we are able to let someone know we care by tone alone. Your empathy will come through clearly with the proper tone. And just as this might be the case, so, too, will it be so that negative emotions or lack of concern will come to the forefront as well. Let's try one: **"We will happily provide you with a wonderful price for this unit, if it is, in fact, one you would like to own."** Say this positively, nicely, and with matter-of-fact tone.

How about the same response to "Gimme your best price."

Say the same words with a tone that indicates you doubt the customer's level of commitment even if you were to give a great price. Hear a difference? You should. Your ability to purposely create a negative tone will help cement the importance of a positive one, so practice. Again, basic example, but point made.

With respect to the final factor, that being *expression* – this one can really be the biggie. Every time we are placed in a position to receive an objection, we begin to sense it. When this happens, it is natural for us to take on a more serious demeanor. As soon as the customer actually objects or disagrees with us, our tension rises and it is again a natural thing for us to appear defensive or irritated. The only way to avoid this is to practice in like situations. Be aware of your facial expression. Try to smile, not a scary, exaggerated, toothy, nut-bag smile, but a natural one. Try to make sure your eyebrows remain unfurrowed and raised slightly – this is more pleasant to your customers.

There are so many different examples of how these things can have an effect on our ability to make our customers comfortable, make the value of our product clear, and help the customer understand what is represented by this value.

Also involved in delivering your words properly is a basic understanding that all personality types can be effectively dealt with using feigned indifference. An example being that you have greeted a dominant or type "A" individual who tries to immediately control the flow of the conversation and take control of the situation, as they like to do... What then? Well, the beauty of Feigned Indifference and the Technique is that can use retreat or pull-back phrases whenever necessary and always seem to cater to your customer's personality. So, back to our Dominant personality... "I want your best price and I want you to appraise my car now! I've only got a little bit of time!" You reply politely, calmly and with an understanding smile, "**Of course, I am at your service. I**

am grateful for your patience. While we are collecting information about your trade … etc. The idea, be nice and let this person know that they are in charge and control. "Hurry up!" an extreme "A" might say. **"Certainly Mr. Johnson. You control what we do here for you."** As this continues, you go about your job the way you know how. "I have to go!" Mr. Johnson says. **"That is entirely your choice. I know your time is valuable. I would be happy to bring you the vehicle of your interest at any time."** Believe it or not, you might find that this person has more time, or you will be able to set up another appointment. The key again is to make them comfortable in your store. And don't worry; you know you will be able to take control when the time comes. The customer has to want to be at your store.

What about the opposite end of the spectrum, the Stable or Analytical type? Well, the same applies: a polite understanding and a calm desire to serve will work with these folks as well. Why? Because, as with anyone else, they want to believe that everything is their decision as well. The only difference might come in the closing questions. To close the type "A" Mr. Johnson, you might adjust your tone a bit to sound a bit more matter-of-fact (practice out loud), **"Mr. Johnson, if you see the value, and I believe you do, why don't we continue with the paperwork?"** The more docile Mr. Johnson could be asked a softer manner (practice this out loud as well), **"Mr. Johnson, if you see the value, and I believe you do, why don't we continue with the paperwork?"** Practice makes perfect. Again, any program that increases your knowledge of personality types is highly recommended. Ultimately, it is up to you to practice the delivery of all your words. It will make a big difference.

The Write-up (Presenting the Numbers)

One of the most important, if not the most important, activities during our vital processes or Road to the Sale is the write-up. We need to get as many customers as we can on paper. We need to present numbers to everyone we can. As a salesperson, we can rarely close a deal without a complete and proper write-up. As with anything else, whatever the procedure at your facility might be, that procedure is to be done consistently, every time all of the time.

The best way get started on the write-up is to come off of the demonstration drive with a trial close of sorts. The purpose behind this, of course, is to apply a barometer to your customers. Where are they in the process? What are their thoughts? Whatever your management team mandates is fine. Here are a couple of solid trial closes that have worked well over the years:

"If everything works out from a financial standpoint, and I'm sure it will, I imagine this is the vehicle you'd prefer to purchase today. Is that right?"

"Please park this over is the sold row."

Summarize, then "It seems we've found the right vehicle for you. Why don't we go inside and complete the paperwork?"

Based on a positive response to a trial close (anything, as long as deemed effective, should be used), you will ask your customer to continue with the paperwork, or some other closing question. We will now assume a favorable attitude on the part of your customer and will proceed to the write-up. A non-favorable position has been addressed a bit earlier, the most common being, "I have to think about it." We will cover counters to other non-favorable positions in the <u>Famous Last Words </u>portion at the end of this chapter.

You are to write up the vehicle in the manner taught by your management team. Whether it is unstructured (writing on a blank sheet of paper), or presented one piece at a time (trade, then payment), or you follow a four-square or modified four-square, the idea is to do it the same way all of the time, every time. Why? Well, with this much practice, we assume we will get really good at it.

We've already discussed how important it is not to take anything personally. Well, here is your opportunity again to show how skilled you have become with respect to having your true emotions written all over your face. No matter how well you have gotten along with your people up to now, you might seem to be building a beautiful friendship, the numbers you are about to present can undo all of this in a heartbeat. It's not a certainty, but be aware of it. And don't let anything take your smile and positive attitude away. You simply counter, using the Technique, until you can take home the sale. Here is an example of how to present the numbers – remember, do not hold them to your chest for any period of time. You are going to have to address objections or concerns anyway. It is always easier to do this if your people have some trust in you.

"Mr. and Mrs. Smith, the vehicle you are purchasing is a brand new _____. It is value-priced from the factory at $22,995. We have added for your convenience the Outdoor and Appearance package for $895. You have the option of a $2,500 rebate or a special interest rate of ___ for the longer term of 60 mths. Based on the information we've shared, all of our sources and the marketplace have ranged your vehicle's value to be between $3,500 and $4,300. We have shown $4,000. This dollar will be allowed if the vehicle rides and drives-out well. With your choice of either 10%, 20%, or 30% down, you have a choice of the following payments at 36 and 48 months. Which works best for you?"

You will now begin getting responses and/or concerns and objections. And, as has been written before, defer to your management team. If you have a different presentation, you will still be able to incorporate all the material in this book.

You may or may not have included additional accessories packages or mentioned special financing. It is recommended, as said before, that lease payments are always a good idea to present when advantageous. And, obviously, a pre-owned vehicle will probably not have accessories or special rates (unless there is a certified program). Just present what is given to you.

And even if the customer says that they want to write a check, you present a payment. Always give them the option. *It will help your conversion percentage.*

One of the biggest objections salespeople have to the four-square, formal or not, is the practice of showing a large down payment and a short-term, higher payment. This is made more difficult if the customer has already voiced their down payment and payment goal. Whether or not your management team uses the four-square to generate an offer or simply to show the numbers in an organized fashion, your job is to present the numbers to the best of your ability. If the purpose is a little more traditional or old-school and you find yourself having to pull your people off of the ceiling, just remember, there are always ways to calm people down, there are always different ways to present things…

Such as, and this is the worst case scenario… Your customer has mentioned the desire to be around $350 per month and your manager sends you back with five thousand down and payments from $475 to $500 per month. What now? Your customer looks flabbergasted, maybe even irate – "Were you not listening when I told you where I wanted to be with my payment?"

"Of course I was listening, John. As always, we like to present the optimum way for our customers to purchase the automobile. Good money down and a shorter term will always put our customers in a better equity position down the road. This being said, I'm sure we can tailor a package just for you."

After calming John down a bit, you will want to solidify him on the trade allowance and then offer some form of option for dollars down.

"How close to this five thousand dollar figure can you come to help reduce your payments to closer to what you have budgeted?"

Again, you get the idea. Utilize all of the material in this book to overcome any and all concerns, item by item. As with anything else, practice will allow you to polish your presentation to the point that it is nearly flawless. You will be able to branch off at any time to counter a concern and close from it. As it all begins to make perfect sense and you improve your ability to make your customers comfortable and understand the numbers, your closing percentage and gross will rise noticeably.

Famous Last Words?

What do we do when we think it's over? Go to the manager? We always have time for that. Remember, when you take it to the limit, it gives us the greatest result, whether it be the sale or gross, or both. WE ALWAYS HAVE TIME TO GO TO THE MANAGER, AND HE/SHE WILL MAKE THE DEAL HAPPEN. IF AT ALL POSSIBLE, IT WILL HAPPEN.

Prior to a closing situation, a customer might want to leave your dealership for any number of reasons, some you will be able to discover, some you won't, and it will require follow-up to find out if you can get them back in. But here are some ideas to provide a little "Be-back dust" as you might have heard it called:

"Thank you," your customer says after a presentation or demonstration or write-up (it can happen at any time), "We are going to keep looking." You must always respond with this...

"I understand. What other vehicles are you considering? I would be happy to provide you with information on those as well." (Competitive Comparison)

What this will do, hopefully, is allow you another shot to show your customer why your vehicle is the one to buy. If not, your customer might give it the ol' "I have to think about it," and we know how to handle this one, right? (pg. 106)

Next is a great one if you are all-in, or believe you are, on anything – price, trade-in, payment, what have you... And they didn't particularly bite on the "I have to think about it" counter.

"What are your options?"

This is particularly effective if the customer says anything at all. Why? Because we have more counters and more opportunity to close from them. "I'll keep my vehicle," the customer says. We counter:

"And risk hundreds or thousands of dollars in repairs when you could be driving a vehicle with warranty? That's not an option, John. Let's continue with the paperwork."

This is just another idea or example of how this question is able to bring us back to something on which we can utilize the Technique and make the sale.

The next idea is what I have defined as the **Fatigue Factor**. This is what can and will occur if our customers shop too long. We are perfectly able to lose a deal to this effect at any time. And, interestingly enough, we might lose a customer who knowingly spends more money at another dealership for the same type of vehicle on which you have sold them. How does it happen? Simple. A customer sets out that morning to buy a car, perhaps a particular car, perhaps not. They come to you, a highly-trained salesperson. You either confirm in their minds that the vehicle they are looking at is indeed what they want, or, you, through superior sales skills have showed your customer that another vehicle would be just perfect, but we can't close them and they leave. They are at the third or fourth dealership. They're tired. They have found an acceptable vehicle, maybe not even the one they'd rather have, but acceptable. The price is close, maybe within a hundred or two. They might not even like the salesperson or dealership as much as you and yours, but they say, "Oh, all right. Let's get this over with." This happens more often than we might believe. We have to be aware of this. And we'd better bring it up as a last resort.

"What I worry about most, Mr. and Mrs. Smith is the fatigue factor. I fear that you'll end up paying more somewhere else simply because you'll be so tired of shopping. It happens..."

If you have not already pre-negotiated at a One-Price facility, please use the following:

"Your time is valuable... Anyone can beat anyone else by 100 or 2. Let's take care of this right now. You're worth it. Shall we then continue with the paperwork?"

This next famous last words idea potentially opens up another dialogue that will allow you to get to the heart of the matter...

"I often ask myself why some buy right away and some don't buy at all... Is it that some buyers understand something that others do not, and, if so, I wonder what that information might be. What are we missing? What have you read or heard that is keeping you from buying this automobile when so many others have?"

Customers need to be comfortable with the salesperson and the facility, understand the value the vehicle represents, and it should be within their budget parameters. If it is not within the budget, they must understand why it is important to pay for it.

Finally, let us revisit Logic vs. Emotion. You must convey to your customer that all sound decisions are made by way of logic and reason. These decisions are made with no emotion - particularly false, negative emotion.

I will end this section and chapter with a short story. I had a wonderful potential customer on the phone to her husband overseas, who owned a company for which she was a partner. Interestingly enough, she was accompanied, in our showroom, by the president of the company. The whole issue was, again, discount. The owner, overseas, had no idea except that he was told there was no discount to be had. He was not aware that there was already a discount and/or incentive on the vehicle, and that they had been shopping everywhere and this was the unit that his wife wanted. His idea, as well as hers was that there is always something to be had. The good old apple story was used as a closing tool. She told me that the managers in her company always interceded and offered something more to close the deal. I told her that I would be happy to come in and train all of her managers. I expressed to her that the negative emotion of not gaining an additional discount on a product that was clearly worth all the money was having an effect on her reasoning. Lose the emotion, I told her. Rational decisions in business or in life are always better than emotional ones. I then, with feigned indifference, offered that if she found a vehicle with more value for less dollars, she should buy it for the good of herself and the company. If not, she should buy what made most sense to her. Ultimately, she committed.

The moral of this is that we must always consider counters during our down time. What ifs should be contemplated at all times, and solutions to these should always be recorded and practiced. If they are effective, use them. If not, abandon them and create new ones. It is up to us to be the best. No one else.

Chapter In-Review

This is where everything should begin to become more and more clear to you. But, you have read through this material. I know that you have started to formulate your own ideas about how all of this will fall together for you. And that is where the fun is born!

1. Practice Your Presentation

Every day we have down time... That is what I hear more complaints about. Why would we be on the internet (unless it is researching competitive information or other training material)? We should be practicing, doing walk-arounds, getting better. I realize it is difficult, but invest in your future: practice, practice, practice.

2. Use Logic To Break Through Negative Emotion.

This is another area that we need to practice more than others. We are going to be bombarded with negatives from our customers. They are protecting themselves, in their minds. Be positive always. Help the customers understand that if a vehicle is what they need, you are the one to find it for them. We cannot compromise a great attitude.

BEYOND THE WALKAROUND

Lead Management and Follow-up

The Big Blue Book was one of the first things I was given when I started in this business. Many of you will remember it as the one of the best ways then to manage leads, record activities and sales, and do follow-up. Many of you probably don't know what I'm talking about. I imagine this blue book is still around in some facilities which have not been upgraded to the advanced CRMs with which a lot of us are now familiar. This blue book might also still be used by any of you who, like me, may have been born a couple-three hundred years too late. You've heard of us... We would far prefer writing things out with a quill and ink, then sealing it with wax and sending it away with a horse or two. And, for those of you who have been around awhile, you will also recall the large, more long really, desk logs where the information of every customer for that day was to be written down. It was from these pages that the consultant and sales manager would have, or should have, had one-on-one sessions in order to keep up to date every month. Some stores also had three-ply registration cards that were used to keep track of all customers. These older methods captured similar information, including where we might have left off on the road to the sale. Just like any process, anything chosen was as good as the other so long as it was used consistently. So whether you use one of these follow-up tools or a more modern CRM – VinSolutions, DealerSocket, ADP, etc. – the goal is the same: collect and save as much information as you can for every customer and sell that customer multiple vehicles over your career. Rely on this information for referral business as well. Every contact is precious to your career and we will learn how to maximize them all.

In this chapter we are going to cover how to handle incoming phone calls and e-mails, how to use both sources for follow-up, and how to stay in touch with your sold and unsold customers.

We really didn't go into detail with respect to the importance of making everyone a contact and keeping a record of every single person. The customer who comes in the front door to grab a brochure and leave is a quality lead. We have to do what we can to capture at least a portion of this customer's information, most importantly the e-mail address. *E-mail capture is now a primary criteria many manufacturers use for grading customer experience.*

There are many dealer groups moving away from traditional marketing and toward direct mail, event marketing, equity-mining and just utilizing the tools within the CRM to more thoroughly work the sales and service owner base. With these you will spend substantially more time on the phone and through e-mail than you have in the past. You should dedicate a minimum of two hours a day prospecting and working your owner base. The highly successful sales consultants dedicate more time than this.

It is understood that those of you new to the business will not have a substantial owner base. This is why every contact is vital. Ask for orphan owners. Once you have convinced your manager that you are able to work and establish results, he or she will gladly help you grow your business in this way.

Before we move forward, you should understand that communication skills as a whole in society are eroding at a dramatic rate. We are leaning more and more toward short, quick communication because of the pace of our lives. Face-to-face conversations take place far less than they have in the past. This is unfortunate because it is the best form of communication. One can experience facial expression and body-language where this is not possible over the phone or by e-mail. The telephone at least gives us tone to go with our words. E-mail gives us neither and is a dangerous form of communication. How often have we read something into an e-mail that was not intended at all? If it can create anger, worry, or hurt feelings among friends, what might be conveyed to our customers if we are not careful?

You would do well to use any means necessary (many good programs out there) to improve your conversation skills. It will be invaluable moving forward. And if you are questioning the congruency of this statement because of the fact that society is going the other way - don't. Just because your customers might be underachieving in this area certainly does not mean that you, becoming highly-skilled, cannot make them feel more comfortable and, as such, more likely to buy from you.

Times have certainly changed. As recently as 150 years ago, we can look back at the writings of the Civil War, the documentation, the communication, the way they wrote and spoke, and clearly see the tremendous decline. Theirs is almost a foreign language today. Aside from the advancements in technology, one from that era would no doubt believe he had traveled backward in time rather than forward. The reading of a modern text or tweet would, more than likely, disgust the traveler as well. Yes, it has gotten bad. Morse code, tribal drums, and smoke signals might be the only forms of communication less effective than e-mail. So, now it's up to us to be better than our competition and be professional with our customers and make them feel more comfortable and more important. This being said, it is not rocket science. There are some simple basics that will allow us to do what we want to do best: get face-to-face with a live customer and sell them a car.

Phone Skills

Unlike some of the phone training one might have heard or studied over the years, we are going to alter the object of the first phone call. Instead of trying to set an appointment, we want to **create a second contact**. This is just the beginning of the process of **engaging the customer**. This will be a theme when we learn the best way to sell over the internet. Here is the premise: the more different and multiple contacts you have with a customer will build a stronger and stronger bond, maybe even a loyalty of sorts. Engage the customer. Don't just give information.

From the beginning... Answering the incoming sales call is much like the welcome for a floor guest.

"Good morning (afternoon, evening). This is Fred."

That simple. With a basic introduction, the common response of the caller is to do the same. Now, many phone skills training programs recommend putting the caller on hold almost immediately in order to break the customer's momentum and gain control of the call. While this is understood, there is a danger of the caller hanging up without us having the opportunity to build any rapport at all. The customer might then call back, but another consultant may get that call - not what we want.

What we want to do is interrupt the caller by calling them by their name, if we get it; and we should most of the time. When the caller gives a name, we respond simply...

"Hi John!"

So the opening is the following:

"Good morning (afternoon, evening). This is Fred."

Caller: "My name is John Johnson and I'm..."

"Hi John!"

I have had customers call in with either service or sales complaints who were completely turned-around from their edge or bad mood just by hearing "hi" with such a positive tone. With respect to a sales call, the positive energy is a must and will go a long way toward a bond and the customer allowing you to take down information.

Moving forward, the customer asks about a certain vehicle.

"I was looking at your used 2012 Honda Accord. What's your best price on that vehicle?

"That is a wonderful vehicle. Let me put my hands on it to make sure it's still here – I don't rely on lists or reports. I know your time is valuable and I wouldn't want to bring you in if it's not available. May I have a contact number and I'll call you right back?"

This, as simple as it is, has a high success rate. We do not try to set an appointment yet, we do not try to sell the vehicle over the phone, and we do not give a price. If the customer does not want to give a number and just says they'll hold, we will respond:

"I'd rather not put you on hold just in case something comes up on either of our ends. I promise I won't abuse the privilege if you provide a number. But, an e-mail would work, if that's easier for you. What would that be?"

Again, what we are looking for is another contact during which we will more actively engage the customer and try to set up that appointment. There is no real trick to working with customers over the phone. There are a number of phone scripts available to you, many within the workings of your CRM. What you have to remember is that we have many very effective word tracks that we have learned in this book that should be utilized both over the phone and the internet. These things have proven to be very productive over the years. If you must provide a price to a customer on the phone (if your facility and management team allow it –always communicate with them), and they have not seen it priced on the internet, always attach one of the positive value statements we have learned. Use pre-emptive strikes. Engage the customer. Here's an example:

"Our prices are, of course, market-based. These vehicles, with this equipment, have been selling very well for a bit more than this. The price of the unit is $15,000. What time this evening would you like to stop by?"

Again, if they are expecting this price, maybe they've seen it on the internet, you will probably be able to secure an appointment. But, if there is a concern, you will use the very same words as if the customer was in the showroom. You are now closing on an appointment. For instance, if the customer says that the price is too high, you will go all the way back to Preparing For Purchase Consultation and attempt to drill down.

"When you say the price is too high, do you mean for the vehicle or more than you wanted to spend today?"

You will then you go down that road until you can secure an appointment. Perhaps the customer states that they can buy one for less somewhere else. We respond the way we have learned...

"John, all the reasons another facility would sell a vehicle like this for less have already been addressed by

us. Whether it be cosmetic or mechanical, I couldn't say."

Based on how the conversation goes, you might say the following:

"We wouldn't want you to find after 20 days , you need brakes. After 30 days, you need tires. That would take away from the experience. You're important to us and we want to take care of you. So what time works best for you this evening?"

You can see now, and will see as you improve and engage your customers in the future, how this is truly a sport as we mentioned some time ago.

Another way to engage the customer is to ask them questions such as **"What are your thoughts?"** or as we have done before to elicit a justification on their part, **"What have you read or heard that helped you come to this conclusion?"** This will be an effective tactic for e-mail correspondence, to be addressed shortly.

The major takeaway here is to understand that the strategies, tactics, and word tracks that we have studied are to be used in any circumstance. We are clearly at a larger initial disadvantage over the phone and even moreso on the internet. Anything we can do to lessen this little uphill battle is important to our success.

What we do not want to do is push and push harder for that appointment on the initial phone call if at all possible. We can certainly go for the appointment on the first call if the customer is reluctant to give out contact information. At that point, it can do no harm.

Understand, though, that if we hammer home the appointment and the customer finally agrees without giving us contact information and the means to tie-down the appointment, what have we created? Absolutely – a *no-show*. So be careful. Use a happy, helpful tone that increases the customer's comfort level and makes them want to deal with you more than anyone else.

One of the more difficult aspects of working with customers over the phone is the introduction of a trade-in. It is truly amazing how many people could possibly expect top-dollar for a vehicle that is still a mystery to the buyer (us). But they do, and we created this also. "Ball-parks" are risky, both because it could lose the deal from the outset, or it could set up a situation where we might be inclined to put too much money in the trade. The best way, obviously, is to get the customer and the trade into the facility. And the most effective manner in which to accomplish this is to interrupt the customer the second a trade is mentioned and ask them to bring it in.

The customer likes the idea of your car, or you've skillfully countered any concerns, and then the trade pops-up: "I also have a 2008 Jeep Commander. I'd like to –" Cut the customer off as soon as you can and happily ask:

"Sounds great! When can you have it here?"

Or the customer begins, "I was wondering how much you would give me for my 2008 Jeep –" Happily, positively cut the customer off and ask the same question or a similar one:

"How soon can you have it here (bring it in)?"

There will be times when a customer will press you on the trade value over the phone. Rather than lose the opportunity, engage the customer. Pull out an appraisal form and begin going over the vehicle with the customer – miles, condition, equipment, everything. Don't be afraid to ask tire depth. Ask everything you would as if the vehicle were on the grounds at your facility. Explain how you will research and share market information with the customer. This will allow you time and the chance to get contact information if you have not obtained it before. *Now we have a direction.*

As we have seen, the phone call is nothing by which to be intimidated, nor do we require an elaborate process.

- Be ready to answer the call
- Maintain a happy and positive tone
- Counter any concerns
- Engage the customer
- Create a second contact
- Build rapport and loyalty
- Set an appointment
- And sell a car.

Internet Skills

As more and more of our traffic is driven by internet, most facilities have introduced a BDC (Business Development Center) or an Activity Center to handle, at least initially, the higher volume of internet leads and requests. Most CRMs have in-depth reports available to tell us a whole host of neat things with respect to our internet productivity. As a sales consultant, you want to initially devote your energy to just a few areas of interest.

1. Number of leads
2. Appointments
3. Appointments Shown
4. Deals Closed
5. Vehicles Delivered

In some facilities, the consultant does not set the appointment, rather the appointments are handled by the BDC and distributed, perhaps, in a round-robin format. If this is so, it is still recommended that the consultants take the time to tie-down or confirm the appointment. Again, there is little worse than a no-show on a busy day when you could be selling a car to someone else. We need to always communicate strongly with our guests. Even though we might not have the early contact in the process, what we are able to accomplish after the fact or if the BDC is not able to set an appointment (these should always be turned-over to the sales staff) will play a large role in our success. When we move on to follow-up, e-mails will play a large roll obviously. But let's focus now on some basic ideas that will help you have the successful appointments.

Internet customers should be worked very similarly to showroom guests and phone-ups, except that, as we recall, this form of communication is least effective and most risky. But these customers must also be engaged. Ask questions. How do they feel about something? What do they think? Keep in mind that the majority of early responses are probably automated. The response will provide a price and maybe other suggestions, like pre-owned options. This package will be wrapped into a nice, generic, formatted response that will produce little in the customer and certainly not engage them. The responses from the facility should be filled with gratitude, respect, and warm fuzzies. You would be surprised to see the customer reaction.

One of the reports, getting back to that, shows how many views and responses are produced by each particular e-mail. So, for instance, a 2nd follow-up e-mail might show 60 views of 100 sent, but perhaps only 7-8 responses. A high percentage of customers have lost interest by this step. Lack of engagement? Probably. You might have dozens of templates available for your use, but if they are not getting responses, what good are they? By utilizing our pre-emptive strikes, our positive value statements, and asking the customers for thoughts and input, you will see a spike in views and responses. This will produce a higher number of appointments and more sold units. So, how do we engage the customer over the internet?

There will be a time to utilize the telephone and call these customers, if a phone number (a good one) has been provided, but I am not a proponent of immediately phoning these people. It is understood that many internet trainers are given to e-mailing a response and calling the customer within minutes. One thing to remember: *If this customer had wanted to make a phone-call and speak with a live person, common sense would dictate that the customer would have made a phone call.* Further, our phone-skills might not have yet been honed to the sharpness we would like. Getting a manager involved (the managers should be monitoring your progress) is a great idea and many of them are extremely good on the phone.

But, let's find a way to engage the customer, get multiple contacts, and set up a time to speak with them on the phone – unless, of course, we are able to set the appointment and confirm it. In any event...

Generally, prices are posted and updated on the internet so customers have a solid idea about that prior to contact. Sometimes, it is considered a starting point for them. We can refer back to the Overcoming Price Concerns chapter for a refresher on some countering word tracks. Either way, you will find that the majority of the new car buyers on the internet will have utilized a buying service of sorts or will have contacted several different facilities. Our job is to get a response, because most of the time the customer ceases communication if the price is deemed to high. Some might even consider it insulting. We need to make a recovery and get an answer back. Here are a couple of examples which have proven to be very effective:

"Hi John,

Thank you for taking the time to contact us regarding the purchase of your new _____. These vehicles have been selling very well for the price we have quoted. Many of our good customers are thrilled that we are able to offer such value. We'd love to have your opinion. Everyone is extremely important to us. Thoughts?"

Or.

"Hi John,

I'd love to hear how the buying experience is going for you. We'd like to have you come in and visit us to learn more of what we have to offer. What does your time-frame look like? I would like to keep you up-to-date on any changes in incentives. Any other thoughts or questions? We are at your service. Have a great day!"

With a bit of luck, we will be able to enter into a conversation with the customer that will build that rapport and bond we mentioned before. Once the exchange begins and the customer becomes comfortable communicating with you, you will be able to utilize the many words we have learned to overcome concerns and create that appointment. Here's a great late effort to bring the customer in:

"All the manufacturers pay the same for the new vehicles. We won't lose a deal over dollars. Come on in John. We'll take great care of you."

Use everything at your disposal. Use the famous last words if you have to. Bring up the fatigue factor if you must. This entire book is filled with ideas to counter, transition, and close. It's not a bad idea to ask if you can set up a phone call at this point.

I remember a situation when a sales consultant was having a heck of a time trying to reign-in an internet lead. The customer was making silly offers every communication, quoting what other dealers were telling her. There was a trade involved and I asked the consultant if we had seen it (I didn't begin the deal with him). He said no. I immediately went in and shot a communication to the customer. I introduced myself, told her we all pay the same for the new vehicles and that everyone is important to us. I mentioned that we won't lose the deal over dollars. And then I simply wrote: "I would love to see your trade. When can you have it here?" She said she could stop by at lunch. She came in and we wrote the deal. The consultant was stunned. After he was done, he asked how I got her to bring the trade in. I asked her, I told him. But, I also made it clear to him that because he had done a good job engaging her and getting multiple responses (internet be-backs), I was able to accomplish that which I might not have otherwise.

Follow-Up

One thing to remember about follow-up: Too little and you lose a car deal; too much and you lose a customer, perhaps more.

Everything we have learned in this book, and will continue to learn through other training material and experience, must get you successfully to the follow-up step – either post-sale or should the customer leave your facility without making a purchase. If you have not created a situation that will lead to purposeful and productive follow-up, you have lost.

With this said, it should be re-iterated that our primary function is to sell and deliver a vehicle as immediately as possible while maximizing all the profit available. If we cannot, however, we simply must have shortened or *eliminated the customer's shopping list*. There have been many cases of shopping lists being so well destroyed by a great experience that the customer never makes it home or to another facility. They simply leave, turn around, and come back to buy the unit. No sales consultant or facility should look at surviving on be-backs, but you'd better create a bunch of them in order to thrive in your marketplace.

No-purchase Follow-Up

If you do not have earth-shattering news, please do not call the customer on their cell phone immediately or even a couple of hours after they have left your facility. It makes you look desperate and unprofessional. And, quite frankly, if you have not done your job building value in your product or rapport with your customer, the short time apart is not going to alter the perception. This is why *being on top of your game every time a customer is in your showroom is paramount.* Everything comes from that performance: An immediate sale or a be-back opportunity.

First follow-up opportunities will indeed take place the same day, however. If your customer has a land-line (I know, fewer and fewer do), you or your manager should indeed call right after the customer leaves. You will leave a message on their machine, if they have one. I know it's a bit old-school, but there should be no prejudice to the oldies but goodies, right? Leave the following message:

"Hi John, Hi Jill. This is Fred calling from (Your Dealership). Thank you again for taking some time to spend with us today. I hope you enjoyed it as much as I did. Please call with any questions. I am at your service. Have a great night."

Practice leaving messages with your teammates or sales manager until they are flawlessly professional. They must have feeling and sincerity.

This message will be sent in conjunction with an e-mail. Remember, we spoke about how important it is to collect these addresses? *Again, e-mail should ultimately be easier to capture than other personal information because it's use is less intrusive.* Anytime you try to take information, please make the customer understand that it will not be abused. Besides, if you are a source of irritation, how likely is the customer to purchase from you? I would use this argument with anyone a bit reticent to give information.

With an initial follow-up e-mail, there are consultants who will even send a *video file* showing the vehicle of interest with another short presentation, perhaps addressing a couple of items that might have been missed. Or the video will provide other options just like some automated e-mails will attach other vehicles in stock (both new and used) that might work for that customer. The purpose of any initial follow-up, whether it be phone, e-mail, or a hand-written thank you card, should be full of warm fuzzies and some new information that will engage the customer and generate the desire for a second, third, or how many other contacts are required to sell the vehicle.

Another phone message might say the following:

"Hi John, Hi Jill! This is Fred from your dealership. I was just thinking about you (guys) and I had a great idea... (and tell them something new or ask for a call back). Definitely something to consider. Hope you're having a great day!"

Post Sale and Owner Base

In our business more and more of the retailers are of the opinion that the facility is responsible for bringing in 50% of the traffic and the consultant is responsible for the other 50%. It seems like a lot to place on the shoulders of your average sales consultant, doesn't it? Not really. And most don't want to be average. Your purchase of this book is an indication that you desire excellence. You have more means today to market yourself than ever before.

I don't recall his name, but a trainer with a recruiting company said something many years ago that really stuck with me. I'm not sure if it was his idea or not, but he said to look at least six customers past each person walking through your doors. That is only the beginning of how valuable every customer is to you and your business. This speaks along the same lines of how precious every contact is to you. It is not just your job to sell each customer, but to provide such a wonderful experience that these customers of yours will tell everyone they know that you and your facility are the be-all, end-all with respect to purchasing their next car or truck. *And this is how you become among the best in the world at what you do.*

In order to bring the majority of your customers back in, to make sure they are consistently sending you the business when available, you and your own contact information must stay in front of them all on a frequent basis.

I recall back again to my early days when there was a gentleman who sold us calendars to send to our customers. They were on simple construction paper. They had cartoons and a theme for each month. And they had our names on them. While our dealership was signed up with him, I remember sending these calendars to every one of my customers. I remember giving remainders to new prospects to help create be-backs. This small item was effective and provided this talented fellow with a pretty decent living back then. Understanding this, can you imagine what you can do as a consultant with the technology available to you today? FaceBook, Twitter, Google + and other, yet to be created, accounts will be even more effective with up-coming generations. Create accounts for your business and ENGAGE the customer. Texts create another opportunity that is less intrusive. Even though I have sold a vehicle nearly entirely (shame on me) through text, if I did not get permission prior, I would ask the customer before utilizing this avenue. The customer might text *you* to initiate the process. Please remember that our word tracks can be used through all methods and they will be effective.

You are able to create your own calendars which can be sent out to your customers as a PDF. This will cost you nothing but your time. You can create newsletters to e-mail to your customers monthly. Again, just your time. Every customer, every contact, should be reminded of you every month, certainly every quarter at minimum. If you accomplish this, you will have no slow months, no slow winters. But, you must remember... Earn the right to constantly contact these people. To do this, their experience must be superior.

Chapter In-Review

1. **Get Contact Information**

The primary responsibility during an incoming sales call is to get contact information and create another contact. Think in terms of creating a be-back over the phone or on the internet. Be-backs have a higher closing percentage than walk-ins. And you will have a higher appointment percentage if you can create multiple contacts.

2. Engage Your Customer

Do more than your competition. Do not just give information and expect great results. Don't try to sell, certainly not oversell, the vehicle over the phone. You do not have proper time or information. Ask questions of your customers. Compliment them on the quality of their questions and the effort they have made to research the purchase. And "hang on their every word." Just like a smile can be heard on the phone, so too can your genuine interest.

Ask key questions over the internet. Be aware of your tone in your e-mails. Read and re-read all of them. If you are unsure, let someone else read it before you send it out. Professional engagement will increase the number of responses, then appointments, then sales.

BEYOND THE WALKAROUND

Conclusion

As we come to an end to this book, the importance of continued education cannot be stressed enough. Nor can the routine of practice. There have been many ideas presented over many years with regard to all sales, not just in the automotive industry. But might it be stated that I really know of no more complex or competitive industry. There are so many options out there. We really need to deal with our customers better than the other consultants. It is the only way to increase our effectiveness.

There are many really good sales training books and programs available that emphasize the potential of this business. Many of them have not changed, however, for decades. This being said, they still have much value. These programs teach goal-setting and activities and what money there is to be made. They paint a very rosy picture, when, in reality, and just like anything else, there are only a select few who excel. Let's quickly take a look at why this might be the case and how we can make it *you*...

My attention was grabbed by a commercial that said something to the effect of "Are you tired of diets that just don't seem to work and often leave you weighing more than you did before?" It struck me because of the ridiculousness of the claim. The diet would have worked wonderfully in most cases, if not all, *if it was followed*. The people failed, not the diet. The diet did not leave people weighing more than before – the people stuffed themselves to make up for the misery of denying themselves all of the food they love for a particular time. And so, too, is it with us. Most of us, myself included at one time, would almost rather do nothing than something that seemed tedious or hard-starting even though it would be of great benefit.

I attended a Brian Tracy seminar in the fall of 2008. I would, again, highly recommend this product. Mr. Tracy is a proven professional and clearly one of the best in the world at what he does. But I was struck by the fact that there were probably 500 people in the room for this seminar and I wondered to myself how many would change or grow from it? What percentage would re-read the material, would listen and listen again to the audio programs in order to improve themselves? 50%? Not likely. 30%? Hmmm. Maybe not even that many. Of course, the best way to sell the value of an expensive seminar certainly did not include the exclamation that not 100% of the audience will use any of the information. Why on earth would I bring this up? I want you to read and re-read this material. It will help you define yourself. Make it your own.

Why did I believe this could be true? Well, I looked at myself, my own history. I had seen Zig Ziegler live and in-person in the late eighties when I was twenty-two or twenty-three. I really didn't pay too much attention, although I thought he was pretty good – aside from sounding like a preacher and telling me how to raise my kids (I didn't have any). I lost the good material soon after that, because, quite honestly, I thought I was too good for it. I have purchased programs by Tony Robbins and seen him live. I rented a Brain Tracy video on selling in the early nineties when I first started in this business. I thought it had some good ideas, but it didn't apply to me and, again, I was better than that. I was smart, I could wing it. I purchased programs published by Nightengale-Conant, programs on how to read people, how to set and achieve goals, how to converse, etc. I'd listen once or twice, then figured I could get by. I read Think and Grow Rich by Napoleon Hill several times. I enjoyed it, loved the fantasy I was able to create, but I never got the real message – success requires not just knowledge but action based on that knowledge.

I did not grow until I humbled myself and realized that hard work is as important as goals, visions, or desires. One can write down all the hopes and dreams and goals one wants to achieve, but nothing, repeat, nothing, comes of this until action is taken. Absolutely nothing.

This being the case, most think the worst part of this business is the so-called "down-time." In truth, the "down-time" is the beauty of this business, because there is so much to be gained. Most professions do not allow for true on-the-job training the way ours does. We can always study, learn, and anticipate. What must we do or say next time that can make us more effective? We can choose to think this way, or we can choose to talk about why we cannot sell the next customer who walks through the door. It's up to you, but it's your job to be a professional every day. All of us have a multitude of skills. Use your knowledge to use this program and, yes, *improve* upon it. Make it yours. Remember, though, that as you improve, practice is necessary. Always have something to say...

Thank you very much for buying this book...

Believe you are the best every day, every time you are in front of a customer. Always believe that you will sell that customer a car.

But, to believe you are the best, you must give yourself the confidence to be the best. Study, learn, and practice all of the time. Use the skills you have developed all of the time, every time. Consistency is vital! Good Luck, and make some sales that no one but you ever would!

Customer Comfort/Consultant Confidence

"Everything we say or do in the facility should be based on these ideas. They are directly proportional. This is to say that as one increases so does the other; as one decreases, so too does the other. It makes perfect sense. If the customer is uncomfortable (this is the case most often), a sales consultant will lose confidence. We all remember a time when we welcomed a customer to our store and felt that they were uncomfortable (i.e. unreceptive, cold, rude, etc.). We would wonder how we could ever get them to allow us to present a product, let alone sell them a vehicle. If we maintained this belief, it would begin a downward spiral ultimately concluding with the customer leaving. However, if we had such a confidence, such a *feigned indifference*, it would increase the comfort level of the customer. This is difficult, but necessary.

Our customers come in on the defensive, either because they have been coached or have had a bad experience in the past. Their goal is to not give us the upper-hand and make us believe they have no interest in our vehicles (feigned indifference on the customer's side). They will tell us they are just looking, really don't need a vehicle, just want a brochure, tell us they have no time, or come up with a number of concerns or objections (we will learn how to counter all of these)."

All The Best,

Rob

INDEX

Active Walkaround 116, 145

Apple Story 109

Appointment 173, 188, 190, 191, 192, 194, 195, 197, 198, 204

Appraisal Form 115, 121, 194

Bank 47, 62, 93, 134, 135, 155, 157, 158

Better Way.............162, 163

Big Blue Book.................185

Body Language ...21, 25, 151

Brag Book 90

Brian Bursell 74

Brian Tracy....................206

Budget 47

Character......20, 37, 38, 151

Columbo 36, 38

Comfort 2, 9, 12, 21, 26, 30, 33, 37, 40, 41, 44, 50, 55, 57, 59, 88, 122, 171, 193, 209

Confidence 2, 8, 11, 16, 21, 23, 29, 40, 41, 50, 60, 67, 85, 95, 98, 102, 120, 125, 127, 208, 209

Contact 35, 62, 186, 187, 188, 190, 192, 194, 195, 197, 202, 203, 204

Counter 5, 10, 15, 16, 30, 41, 42, 46, 56, 59, 60, 71, 73, 75, 77, 78, 79, 88, 90, 91, 92, 93, 94, 97, 105, 110, 111, 119, 123, 125, 130, 131, 134, 136, 137, 139, 141, 143, 152, 153, 155, 156, 157, 175, 178, 179, 198, 209

Credit Union 56, 63, 134, 135, 157, 158

Customer Comfort 5, 14, 32, 44, 66

Dan Marsh 105

Dennis Snow 20

Directly Proportional 41, 60, 209

Disney 18, 19

Down-time 207

Emotion 2, 55, 137, 167, 168, 181, 182

Environment 14, 52, 53

Evidence manual 90

Expression 10, 11, 20, 29, 67, 75, 132, 159, 167, 172, 187

Expression 168

Failure 23, 24

Famous Last Words 16, 79, 178

Feigned Indifference 13, 15, 41, 65, 66, 80, 83, 106, 172

Five Statements........51, 108

Follow-Up......i, 16, 199, 200

Half-a-Car...............162, 163

Individuality 11, 76, 79

Inflection........167, 168, 170

Interest Rates ...60, 148, 157

Internet Skills.................194

Interview 62

Isolation 9

Jay Dowthard.................137

Jon Meacham 46

Just looking 32, 37, 88

Leasing...........161, 163, 164

Leonard Schmidt..............66

Mind-set Change ..12, 37, 84

Monroney........................90

Nightengale-Conant 207

No-Show.................193, 195

One-Price 7, 52, 53, 62, 78, 79

One-Price statements 51

Owner Base 202

Pay-off 47

Personally 10, 27, 50, 67,
   68, 70, 71, 75, 84, 151,
   175

Phone Skills....................188

Positive Value Statement
  44

Product Presentation 1, 4, 5

Professional 204

Professionalism 118

Rate................165, 167, 168

Reason 11, 29, 55, 73, 74,
   80, 86, 87, 94, 95, 97, 98,
   100, 108, 110, 123, 125,
   126, 137, 139, 142, 147,
   150, 170, 181

Rejection.........23, 24, 36, 67

Science 6, 23, 188

Silent Walkaround 116

Smile and Wave 6, 25

SPACED 46

Sport...........23,

Steven Wiley.....................12

System................. 22, 49, 83

Tax Savings 136

Technique 7, 9, 10, 13, 15,
   32, 60, 65, 69, 70, 73, 74,
   77, 79, 80, 83, 86, 87, 92,
   97, 106, 121, 124, 130,
   133, 139, 140, 144, 153,
   172, 175, 179

Think and Grow Rich......207

Thomas Jefferson 46

Tim Porter........................57

Time-frame 48

Tone ....i, 14, 18, 167, 168

Tony Robbins 207

Transition 89, 91, 115, 120,
   198

Unleashing Excellence 20

Value 6, 11, 15, 22, 33, 34,
   43, 44, 47, 50, 60, 62, 72,
   73, 76, 77, 78, 79, 84, 88,
   89, 90, 91, 95, 96, 97, 98,
   99, 104, 107, 108, 110,
   113, 119, 122, 126, 128,
   131, 134, 135, 136, 138,
   139, 140, 141, 144, 147,
   148, 149, 150, 153, 155,
   170, 172, 173, 176,

181,182, 191, 194, 196, 197, 200, 205, 206

Video 201, 207

Video file 201

Warm Fuzzies 30, 31, 44

Word Tracks 11, 25

Zig Ziegler 206

www.ingramcontent.com/pod-product-compliance
Lightning Source LLC
Chambersburg PA
CBHW070518200326
41519CB00013B/2847